The Earth Manifesto

Thinking Outside the Flocks

by B. H. Roberts, M.Div.

PublishAmerica
Baltimore

First printing

PublishAmerica has allowed this work to remain exactly as the author intended, verbatim, without editorial input.

ISBN: 1-60813-872-0 (softcover)
ISBN: 978-1-4489-0427-3 (hardcover)
PUBLISHED BY PUBLISHAMERICA, LLLP
www.publishamerica.com
Baltimore

Printed in the United States of America

Enjoy the Journey, [signature]

The Ancients believed in the Earth, guided by rational thought and understanding. They knew the Earth was at the center of all. They feared nothing.

The man-made religions have indoctrinated the sheep into accepting a contrived system of superstitious doctrines and coercive dogma as the center of all. They are taught to fear and suffer guilt.

As long as there are sheep, there will be ego-driven shepherds to tend the flocks and see to it that they are sheared and fleeced regularly.

As long as the sheep keep ignoring the Earth to do the bidding of the shepherds, the Earth energy will continue to elude them, and they will remain sheep: undisciplined, irresponsible, irrational, and dependent.

The sheep fear the Earth and all her powerful energies. The shepherds reinforce the fear to maintain the flock's dependence.

The Earth-centered ones know and understand. They are one with the Earth, and have no fears.

The Earth Manifesto

Thinking Outside the Flocks

Introduction

For over 100,000 years, thinking, inventive, tool-using, imaginative humans have populated the Earth. The last Ice-age, which ended about 16,000 years ago, depleted the world population to within a few thousand of any species' extinction level, for those that did survive. Many species did not survive.

It is difficult to divide Earth history into well-defined eras because the changes are so gradual as to be imperceptible, with one blending into the next, and because each category develops at a different rate than the others. For instance: literature, science, art, architecture, economy, industry, and of course, politics, and religion, each has eras of amazing growth and profound retardation. One area will lead as others lag behind, then the later will experience a spurt of energy. Often one will influence another, such as science aiding the military development and promoting a political surge. But the divisions are real and help define the history.

It was in the middle ages when the man-made religions first developed their stranglehold on the population, a time of great unrest. That large period from the barbarian invasions of 375 A.D., or the fall of the western Roman Empire of 476 A.D., all the way to the arrival in America by Columbus in 1492, or the beginning of the Protestant Reformation about 1517, when Luther made his ideas known. This entire era is divisible into three rather distinct parts: 1) the transition period from about 375 A.D. until about 800 A.D. could well be called "the Dark Ages". The barbarian hordes were invading everywhere, and those coming from the area of Germany were mixing with the Roman Empire and becoming one people. At the same time the remains of the classical civilization, influenced by the art, literature, architecture, politics, and science of Rome under the likes of Julius Caesar, and all who followed him; was mixing with the culture of the Germanic barbarians, and the early Christians, following the dictates of Constantine, and all was fusing to become medieval Europe. 2) What was usually called Middle Age starts with Charlemagne before 800 A.D., as he tried to revive the Western Empire, and runs thru about 1300, encompassing feudalism, the Crusades, and the Inquisition when the religions and their mechanisms tried to run every aspect of human life, which caused some large disagreements between Popes and Emperors. 3) Then there was a time of further transition covering from 1300 until about 1500: the Renaissance. A time when men were expanding their way of thinking more freely, and most categories: art, literature, architecture, industry, and social awareness expanded as never before, developing into new forms and giving politics some serious growing pains.

Earth geography has a huge effect on the way people are able to function and greatly affects their ability to expand thru trade or war. Mountains and oceans act like walls and tend to separate, while rivers and lakes tend to unite.

History is founded upon three primary sources: 1) material remains like ruins, coins, monuments, tools, weapons, and utensils; 2) official documents and descriptions by eyewitness testimony; and 3) oral or written traditions, often from a secondary source, not related to first-hand knowledge. But no matter how important an event may have been, if there is no trace of it, it is as if it never happened and there is no knowledge of it. Sources for the Middle Ages were extremely sparse and included annual chronicles, written by monks, describing the events of the day; written decrees and agreements of Charlemagne and the successive Carolingians, called 'capitularies', along with other collections of laws; charters conveying land and privileges; some few letters to and from kings, popes, and other men of status; life stories of saints and other notable persons written by monks; as well as accounting ledgers and other records from monasteries, municipalities, and land holders. Present day historians are able to find an unending deluge of information from a plethora of paperwork. From parliamentary dockets, congressional records, newspapers, municipal ledgers, diaries, and a host of other sources, an historian can find a description of just about anything. However, the process of slowly and painstakingly sifting thru the material to define the true from the false will often reveal that a newer version has appeared to try to denounce the older one and often becomes the accepted version until someone discovers an older version and reveals the time-tested truth and is able to usurp the usurper. The man made religions have sought to hide the real truth behind their pretended facade of holiness and sanctity as they promote their historically-habituated, superstitious fantasy as reality, often writing their own 'historical documentation' to agree with their agenda.

Sources for this work were some of the oldest historical writings available. some in reprint editions, and some too fragile to be viewed except on microfilm. Most were not included in any history books that were available to our teachers as they struggled to teach the 'accepted' history, fed to us from books written to express someone's agenda because throughout the centuries, people seeking to learn were taught a politically and religiously corrected version of what someone thought they should learn.

History is overloaded with systems of determining time used by different people through all the ages. The Romans started theirs from the founding of Rome, about 509 B.C., then again under Julius Caesar; the Christians start from the birth of Christ (1 A.D.), but miscalculated and threw it off by about 4 years because it was decided about 300 years after it was supposed to have happened; the Mohammedans start from the flight of Mohammed (the Hegira, in 622 A.D.); many kings and popes have used the years of their reigns; and the church of Rome had over 2000 saints' days from which to chose.

The religions influenced the determination of the length of the year. The 'Julian' calendar, contrived by Julius Caesar, which made every fourth year a leap year, was used by many nations until the Middle Ages. But this made the year eleven minutes and fourteen seconds too long, and by the sixteenth century, the accumulated difference since the Council of Nicea (325 A.D.) totaled almost ten days. The improved design of the Gregorian calendar, proclaimed as the correct calendar by Pope Gregory XIII, in 1582, not only removed ten days from that year (October 4 was followed by October 15), but also removed three leap days in every four centuries from then on, providing a future calendar in sync with the solar year. England did not accept the improved calendar until 1752. As it became adopted in various countries, the beginning of the year was set as January 1. Prior to that, the beginning was set as the feast of the Annunciation (March 25), near the Vernal Equinox, and various other dates, so before it was adopted in England in 1752, it was hard to determine whether a date between January and March was part of the previous year or part of the new year. It had to be confusing, when, during the year dates were usually fixed by referring to some church festival like Christmas or Easter, or one of the many saints' days.

The Mohammedan year is a lunar year about eleven days shorter than the Gregorian year, such that 34 Mohammedan years equal about 33 Gregorian years.

For over two hundred years after Julius Caesar and Augustus redesigned the Roman Republic into the Roman Empire, it became the standard by providing unity of government, law, language and a prosperous culture to the Mediterranean world. There followed a century of decline after the death of Marcus Aurelius until the rise of Diocletian, marked by civil war and cultural decay, from 180 – 284 A.D. When Diocletian ascended the throne, he began remodeling the empire, and it continued under Constantine the Great, who died in 337. The empire was divided into an eastern (and western after 395), each section was ruled by a despot, and the capital was moved to Constantinople. Constantine ended the persecutions of the Christians, and made Christianity the official, join-or-die religion of the empire.

The changes helped, but the decay continued due to: 1) a huge decrease in population caused by lack of sanitation awareness, famines, wars, and pestilence; 2) unwise laws concerning taxes written by weak, greedy men in positions of power because of their birth, causing freemen to become serfs, bound to the soil; 3) widespread luxury and immorality enjoyed by the same weak, greedy shepherds; and 4) a lack of nationalism: no feeling of pride and belonging, because despotic rulers hired barbarians into their armies and gave them land to live on, creating a welfare-style system. The shepherds, the ones in control of the population of sheep, were more concerned with their own well-being and cared little for the population except as a source of taxation or service. Every time a shepherd would decide that some other pasture looked greener than his pastures, he would attack a neighboring region.

By the end of the fourth century, the decline accelerated as entire nations of Germanic barbarians entered the Roman Empire, following the previous mercenaries that were hired to do the dirty work the Romans felt they were too noble to do. The Visigoths were being attacked by the Huns from Asia, so they crossed the Danube wilderness, overran and killed Emperor Valens at Adrianople in 378, and following their young king Alaric they attacked Greece and Italy and sacked Rome in 410. Under Alaric's successors they established a Germanic kingdom in Spain and southern Gaul which lasted until 711. This example was followed by others. The Vandals overran Gaul and Spain and when the Visigoths got to Spain, they left for Africa about 429 and remained in charge there for about one hundred years. The Franks came from the lower Rhine region and occupied northern Gaul. The Burgundians came from the middle Rhine region and occupied the Rhone valley until 534. The Anglos and Saxons (Vikings) invaded Britain from 449 and established communities which later consolidated into the kingdom of England. In 451 the Huns raided into the center of Gaul but were repelled by the combined efforts of Romans and Visigoths, and two years later, after the death of Atilla, "the scourge of god", Europe was free of attacks for a while. The shepherds and their flocks settled into new pastures, until they got restless and started the attack process again.

The western Roman empire collapsed in 476, when the leader of the German mercenaries in the Roman army, Odoacer, deposed the young Romulus Augustulus, and assumed the title of 'king', and so informed the Eastern Emperor at Constantinople. By 493, Odoacer was murdered by Theodoric the Great, of the Ostrogoths. Theodoric had come to Italy with his community of sheep and was commissioned by the Eastern Emperor to overthrow the usurping Odoacer.

Theodoric (493 – 526) grew up in Constantinople and hoped, one day, to unite his sheep with that of the Italian provinces into one grand flock. The effort failed due mainly to religious differences: the Ostrogoths, like most German barbarians of the day, were Arian Christians, considered a heretical sect; while the orthodox Roman Catholicism prevailed and thrived throughout the Roman Empire.

The Emperor Justinian (527 – 565) enhanced and strengthened the Eastern Empire while profoundly influencing the West. He was a builder and wise statesman, who codified Roman law into the "Code, Digest, and Institutes" which held great influence in preserving and promoting civilization into the 20th century.

With his generals, Belisarius and Narses, Justinian conquered the Vandal kingdom in Africa in 533 and the decaying Ostrogoth kingdom of Italy in 553. For yet a while the Roman Empire ruled over Italy, southern Spain, northern Africa, and the islands of the western Mediterranean, this was the last time its power was to extend so far.

The start of the 7th century was marked by the growth of a new man-made religion, which, like all others, was also a political/social/military influence. The teachings of Mohammed (571 – 632), united the loosely organized Arab factions, converted them from the worship of 'sticks and stones', and taught them to worship the 'one true god' (Allah) for whom Mohammed was the main prophet/mouthpiece/head shepherd. The teaching of Mohammed was contained in the Koran, their bible, which embodied many Jewish, Christian, and Persian theologies, some noble ideals, and many baser concepts tainted and twisted by the ignorance, cruelty, and sensuality of the naive Arab mind.

By 631, Mohammedanism was the way of life for the entire Arab world, and they entered upon a fanatical zeal and lust for conquest and rule of foreign lands that had not been seen before. These shepherds were out to own and rule the world. In 80 years Mohammedanism conquered more land than Rome had conquered in 4 centuries. Syria, Persia, Egypt, northern Africa, and Spain fell under the rule of the caliphs, the successors of Mohammed; but in Gaul, in 732, the Mohammedans were stopped by the Franks under the direction of Charles Martel at the battle of Tours. This defeat caused the rampant internal conflicts and dissensions within the Arab confederacy to come to a boil and collapse their desire for conquest, and saved Europe from any further encroachment.

After the conquest of the Ostrogoths, another Germanic flock, the Lombards arrived in Italy, replacing them. Soon the Lombards had conquered most of northern Italy, which bore their name, and a large portion of the peninsula. The Eastern Emperors still controlled the main area around the river Po (Exarchate of Ravenna), and the district of Rome (Ducatus Romanus), and the southern points of the peninsula. The main result of the Lombards incomplete conquest of Italy was the formation and growth of a new temporal power vested in the Pope, who, as bishop of Rome, was the head of the Christian church.

Despite the fierce hatred and loathing between the Lombards and the Romans, the Lombards gave up their Arianism and accepted Roman Catholic Christianity. Due to the distance from and the weakness of the Eastern Emperors, the power in the city of Rome gradually passed into the hands of its bishops or Popes, of whom Leo I. (440 – 461) and Gregory I the Great (590 – 604) were most notable of this era. In 729 the Emperor decreed against the use of images in worship, causing the Iconoclastic

Controversy, during which the Pope dissolved his allegiance to the Emperor. At about the same time the Lombards were conquering the Exarchate of Ravenna (727), and it seemed that the Pope ignored the rule of the Emperor just about the time he was coming under the control of the hated Lombards, but was saved by appealing to another Germanic flock, the Franks.

The Franks king, Clovis (481 – 511) had created an enduring foundation by consolidating them under his rule and conquering the neighboring factions. By 561 most of Gaul and the Rhine valley were under Frankish control, and stayed that way for a few centuries. The son of Charles Martel, Pepin the Short, seized the throne in 751 with the help of Pope Zacharias, and was twice asked to attack and subjugate the Lombards under the direction of the Pope. The second time (756) he forced the Lombard king to yield hostages, pay tribute, and surrender the Exarchate at the mouth of the river Po, which he then gave to the Pope, making the Pope a secular ruler. The Pope became a world ranked shepherd by securing the old imperial regions in central Italy under his control. This established a close connection between the Frankish monarchy and the papacy for a long time to come.

By 800 the barbarian invasions were about done. The church was gaining a position of supreme power. Feudalism was creating social order out of chaos by following a similar pyramidal format of the new religion. Many doctrinal disputes concerning the fundamentals of Christianity were arising between the East and the West, and differences about worship and discipline lead to the ultimate rejection by the East of much of the religion of the West.

Scandinavia was starting to become defined as Norway, Sweden, and Denmark and they continued to worship their pagan gods. The pagans that had settled into the British Isles had been Christianized under threat of death. Northern Spain had some small splintered Christian regions which grew over the next seven centuries into a powerful monarchy that drove the Mohammedans out of their country.

When Pepin the Short died in 768, he was succeeded by his sons Carloman and Charles the Great (Charlemagne), who ruled jointly until the death of Carloman in 771, afterwhich Charlemagne ruled alone for 46 years (768 – 814). For more than 200 years the Franks had been involved in an ongoing war with the heathen and barbarous Saxons dwelling in the dense forests, swamps, and vast plains on the North Sea between the rivers Elbe and Ems. Charlemagne was determined to end the conflict by Christianizing and subjugating the barbarians, but it took 30 years to accomplish (775 – 804) and included nine rebellions, and was marked by the worst act of cruelty of his reign when in 782 he ordered the massacre of 4500 prisoners. The most troublesome clans and tribes were transported, en masse, to other parts of the empire. Throughout the region, fortresses and bishoprics were established and provided bases for the first real towns. Christianity was forced upon the population at sword point with laws so strict that converts who ate meat during Lent were condemned to death unless absolved by a Christian priest. Political and religious opposition was eliminated and an enforced peace was observed.

The powerful Lombards continued to be a thorn in the side of the papacy, and when the Pope asked Charlemagne to intervene against king Desiderius in 773, he completely conquered and subjugated the Lombards and took the iron crown, the circlet of which was reputed to have been made from a nail from the Crucifixion. He then renewed the gift his father gave the Pope of the temporal rule of Ravenna and other parts of Italy. The conquest of Lombardy and the donation of the papal states to the Pope influenced Christianity in two ways: it cemented the relationship between the Pope and the Frankish kings and started the revival of the Western Empire on a Germanic basis.

Charlemagne held the reins over most of Europe by 800, and he was the supreme authority over the 'eternal city" of Rome by virtue of the title "Patricius" endowed upon him by the Pope. His sovereignty extended over church and state in spite of the fact that he could not write, though he could read and speak Latin and German and understand Greek. He became the single most influential person on the Earth at the time, strengthening both the Papacy and the Empire.

It is understandable how the vast majority of the population, being forced to choose between the man-made religion of the region or death, found themselves becoming spirited supporters of the religion, inducting their children and their grandchildren, and their children, and so on for generations, up to and including the present. For thousands of years, most humans have allowed themselves and their children and their children's children to be held under the control of various shepherds and treated like sheep, as the man-made religions contrive to control the masses, herding them into flocks, brainwashing them, and turning them into mindless robotics, that have no concept of the powerful ebb and flow of the Earth and its energies. About 10,000 years ago, the ancient pagans understood and revered the Earth, to the extent that they worshipped it. But for the past 1700 years or so mankind has given themselves over to the man-made religious corporations; their lives, money, and even their infant children, before they are old enough to decide for themselves.

Throughout time, mankind has had a strong desire to be a part of something much greater than themselves. The planet we live on is a great mystery which has continued to elude their comprehension. The man-made religions have attempted to address this phenomenon, but have fallen short and have instead succumbed to the ego-satisfying format of a very profitable business selling emotional stimulation of the senses to their flocks. They have conditioned their flocks to accept these stimulations as comfort and a sense of salvation to those who suffer from fears, anxiety, guilt, and despair which the man-made religions continue to inflict on them. These are the sheep; members of flocks, which are lead by ego-centric shepherds, whom the sheep trust, blindly and totally, with too many of the decisions of their lives.

Herein are the means of identifying these man-made religions, how the sheep came to become members of the flock, and what they can do if they prefer to think for themselves and decide to free themselves from the flock mentality. When a person's thinking ability and true knowledge is retarded by the child-like behavior taught by the man-made religions, it takes the form of community-driven bondage that seems escape proof. These sheep have the right to know what sort of subtle conspiracy binds them; mind and body, though few ever apply their intellect to realize how blind and deaf they have become to the sham reality in which they are living.

Once they are awakened to the reality of their situation and have escaped, they are able to find comfort in the truth of how reality actually works, and they can finally realize it has nothing to do with rituals and sacraments or shepherds in fancy robes and funny hats, teaching them to blindly follow their prescribed set of required superstitious activities. They may even come to the understanding that reality has to do with the Earth and how they have been mistreating and abusing it for generation upon generation, and how to reverse the trend by recycling the sheep back into useful, thinking, members of the human race, accepting the direction that the Earth energy is demonstrating.

About 10,000 years ago, after the end of the last major ice age, as the Earth was thawing and returning to a warmer state, groups of Earth-focused intellectuals were developing communities by building megalithic, protective structures to keep track of the seasonal cycles and to pay homage to the Earth. Having just survived an ice age that nearly depleted the Earth's population, they were very aware of the fragility of life, and knew that those who lived under ground shared with them the uniqueness of having survived. The ancient Druids, Aborigines, and others, like the American Indians, had long paid close attention to the weather, animals, trees and plants, and the sky, because they knew their existence depended upon all of it, not just some aspects of it. They understood that all the different parts of the whole had important cause and effect influence upon the interrelatedness of the way life on this planet functions in a cooperation of all the parts that make up the whole.

Those who had survived that ice age carried with them a deeply inbred concern for their survival. The intensity of the extinction level event had such a profound impact upon the human mind and psyche, that it became a part of human genetic composition and remains a serious fear for most of the world's population. A fear of not only personal death but of the end of the Earth is a real part of human nature for many sheep that has been passed on thru the generations giving the shepherd/ entrepreneurs an ingrown fear upon which they have built their contrived empires of fantasy faith and superstitious security that they sell to the sheep as they shovel it down their throats.

Before man-made religions, the ancient 'pagans' were the best informed and tuned-in of the pre-literate world. They honored and worshipped nature and all the natural aspects of the Earth. They knew the ebb and flow of all the natural cycles of weather, seasons, animals, planting and harvest, life and death, calm and storm, light and dark, warm and cold. It was not merely a belief or religion for them; it was their way of life. They had a firm grasp of reality, and knew how cause and effect made the world what it is. Since they depended upon the Earth for everything, it was extremely important to understand the world they lived on and to be able to cooperate with it rather than try to control it. They knew, and accepted, that they could not control it so it was vital to learn all they could about it to be able to not only survive, but to thrive. They lived and prospered by the knowledge they developed over thousands of generations by listening, watching, and learning what their world had to teach, and by respecting and honoring the Earth, the elements, and knowledge.

The pagans built many efficient and effective structures, not only to live in, but to serve as calendars and seasonal observatories to guide their way of life. They learned the natural remedies and cures that were available in their environment: herbs, roots, plants, mixtures, poultices, as well as some rudimentary massage and manipulation. They were a logical, rational people of intellect, living in a harsh, unforgiving world of raw elements that threatened and challenged them daily.

As the world became more populated, the simple, natural ways of the pagans were polluted by the myth-based fantasies of the superstition-driven, man-made religions that forced their beliefs upon the naive mentality of the Middle Ages, tapping into their base fears and promoting an emotional stimulation that kept their minds from thinking, to control their lives and increase the prosperity of the shepherds. To better enable the transition, some of the ancient ways were mixed into the superstitious rituals to make them more acceptable to the population, as the old ways were dissolved away. Soon it was an offense, punishable by death to practice any of the old "pagan" ways.

The ancient ways were swallowed up and lost, overwhelmed

by the new superstitious rituals and man-made fantasies. The old focus on Earth-based reality had taught them truth and confidence in their world, where they had no irrational fears, but a healthy respect for the Earth and the environment, and understanding through logic and reasoning. They became controlled by the invented, fear-based system the new religion was shoveling down their throats, even though it made no sense to rational, intelligent people.

The man-made religions were so afraid of the logical, rational, intelligent, and self-confident 'pagans' that they could not control with their pretended piety and superstitious systems, that they had their flocks kill them to prevent the sheep from being infected by rational intelligence of a thinking mind, which would neutralize and reverse the shepherd's brainwashing, making it ineffective.

The pagan's knowledge and real self-confidence made the shepherds look foolish, (as if the funny hats and robes were not funny enough), because they would not be controlled by the invented fears and pretended 'holiness' being forced upon the world. As the man-made religions grew in size and power, the intelligent 'pagans' went into hiding and held onto their Earth-based knowledge, watching from the sidelines as the Earth and the world populations fell into the greedy, self-serving ways of the greatest scam of all—man-made religions.

As these invented religions grew, they were totally dependant upon the community for all of their needs, since they produced no product. The community was scared into giving them whatever they asked for in exchange for the superficial feeling of security. The people relied upon these charlatans for their peace of mind, which was often shaken when the shepherds invented a new danger to create and maintain a level of fear in the flock in order to fleece them of more food, clothing and riches to appease the shepherds. They were given the best the community had to offer, and it was easy to spot the shepherds because they stood out from the crowd, wearing the nicest robes, the funniest hats and lots of jewelry: the beginning of pontificalia (look it up). The top shepherd always wore the finest robes, the funniest hat, and had a driver for his rock-proof ox cart.

Before 400 B.C. the Greek philosopher, Socrates (469 – 399 B.C.) began a conversational (dialectical) search for truth wherein he found that knowledge was good and would lead to truth. His main pupil, Plato (427 – 347 B.C.), continued the search for knowledge and truth and found it inexorably linked to reason, logic and reality. He founded the Academy in 387 B.C. which remained a center of knowledge and philosophical activity until 529 A.D. They passed the knowledge down; by the old teaching the young what was learned in the past and how to learn for themselves by paying attention to the sky, the water, the earth, and fire: the elements. They learned a respect for all living things…especially the elements and the Earth. They understood that everything was alive and therefore worthy of respect.

After Plato died in 347 B.C., the Academy began to emphasize the moral aspects of philosophy and de-emphasize the knowledge, learning and reason aspects. They developed what became Platonism, a bastardized morphing of philosophy that spun from the purity of Plato's style of thought. They had felt the aura of respect and fear that was looming around them as the rest of the ignorant world looked up to them for guidance, and rather than help people learn how to think they taught them how to behave; the same way Pavlov taught his dogs. Like the proverb says; if you give a person a fish, you feed them for a day, but if you teach them to fish, you feed them for a lifetime. The shepherds had decided to avoid teaching the sheep how to think and discovered how to get them to keep coming to them for their daily feeding, and to make the sheep pay for every step of the process.

During the first century, it is rumored that a minor municipal employee, with an overactive ego, charged with persecuting the large religious sect that threatened the peace and stability of the fledgling Roman Empire, came up with a plan. In his desire to help the empire control the vast multitude of people and deflate the growing discontent threatening the new empire and its emperor (Augustus), he infiltrates the group. This mythical spin-doctor claims to have had a miraculous encounter with the god of the peaceful prophet, who no longer led the group, wherein the god provided him with visions, guiding him to lead the prophet's flock. He claimed to have been converted to their way of belief, and then he proceeded to twist and spin it into his way of belief which happened to match the agenda of the empire. So he defuses the problem, and, by spin-speaking, twists and morphs the peaceful religion into one that became, by 380 and then again about 790, the means of enforcement of the empire's wishes upon the whole known world. To refuse to obey was fatal. This self-sustaining virus continued to thrive well into the 21st century, infecting millions of unsuspecting people. But let us not get too far ahead of ourselves.

By the end of the 3rd century A.D., ancient philosophy was turning away from rationalism and the self-sufficiency of wisdom, with more emphasis on what humans desired and what would satisfy the emotions and the physical yearnings. In other words, what would make humans less fearful and feel more comforted; so they could infect them first with that which they feared and then comfort them with the balm of salvation. Religion became big business. They hit on the notion of selling to the flocks the concept of a kindly-grandfather-in-the-sky-who-was-always-watching-over-you type of god, that was all-powerful, all-knowing, and all-everything who could give humans the solution for all their problems: salvation of eternal life, since they had convinced them that their main fears were related to death. These were the basic building blocks of Paul's Christian thought from the end of the 1st century as the philosophers focused more on the emotional and away from the rational. A thinking sheep was no longer a sheep, and that had to be avoided at all costs.

During the 1st century, it was taught that the god was totally transcendent, not of the world, and was so totally powerful and all-everything that he could only touch the world via his angels. This was an Old Testament rip-off by Philo (25 B.C. – 45A.D.), a Jewish/Hellenistic philosopher of Alexandria who wrote so much that he is probably responsible for the majority of the thought that became Christianity. He expanded upon the Platonic idea of the Logos as the second god, which was morphed into the son of the god which maintained the family imagery. Philo also taught his invented idea that the human spirit could be released from the body only with the help of the god, at death, and that the spirit would go through a process, a series of stages, until it reached godliness. This is probably where Dante got the idea for his "Inferno", and the Church of Rome, its idea for purgatory. It becomes very obvious that men invented religion for their own glory.

Then comes Octavius Augustus, the grand nephew of Julius Caesar, born in 64 B.C. who became the first Emperor of Rome in 27 B.C. until 14 AD. This is most likely when and why they started keeping count of the years, sometime during the reign of Gaius Julius Caesar Octavianus, his emperor name, because this was the extent of the known world and it was the Roman Empire, and he was the first emperor. He could do whatever he wanted. They were still working with the Julian Calendar that his great uncle, Julius, designed, which was not yet refined into the Gregorian calendar (1582). Under the Roman emperor Constantine (306 – 337), who had been a pagan all his life, the new Pauline Christianity was becoming a strong political influence, threatening to split the empire. But as a consummate politician, Constantine allowed more and more toleration of Christianity, and probably made a deal with the cult leaders to say that the new calendar was started on the year that Christianity's main man, Jesus, was born, and even then they missed getting it exact, because it was too far in the past. It was more important to save and maintain the empire than to squabble over what event was to be the honorary starting point of the calendar. He never cared much for Octavian anyway, and he made big points with the new powerful cult: Christianity. He made so much effort to suck up to them that he allowed himself to be baptized on his deathbed, a truly political gesture since only the Christians would believe in it, and it calmed the calamity.

Then there was Theodosius I, The Eastern Roman Emperor from 379, who made Christianity the sole official religion of the empire and forbade other worship forms, thereby establishing Christianity as the join-or-die religion of the known world. This was again reinforced by Charlemagne before 800.

Through the centuries, the religions became as diverse as the people that created them and those who added their own special twists. Those seeking to reconcile religion with nature, came up with Deism; a rationalistic focus trying to de-emphasize the god aspect while leaving it as a main aspect, and Theism; a more philosophical and natural theology with the personified 'grandfather' still in charge of everything, and Pantheism; a really vague idea that equated the whole universe with the god (everything is god). The intellectuals were demonstrating their frustration with the same old dinosaur dumplings the man-made religions were shoveling down the throats of the sheep, and yet they only sought to adjust the religion. They could not see beyond the superficiality of it and could not let go of the concept of the personified god watching over the world because they too had been scared into believing since childhood.

The shepherds developed all sorts of contrivances with emphases on demons and salvation in order to continuously infect the sheep with enough fear and guilt to make them come and do whatever they told them to do. Their way of teaching has always been more of a propaganda-filled, brainwashing process, filled with extensive details on how to perform the special rituals, prayers and day-to-day behavior for the appeasement of the shepherd, and enough fear and guilt promotion to keep them coming back for more, all the while requiring the bringing of offerings to help remodel the shepherds' house or pay for a newer and bigger ox cart to do the shepherd's work or get the shepherd to the golf course on time.

Man-made religions maintain and reinforce their supervisory, regulatory, and disciplinary control over their flocks through an emotion-based system of subjective customs and rituals, designed to control the daily activities of the sheep, all the while avoiding the rational, knowledge-based thought processes of objective reality. The shepherds control the behavior of the flocks rather than let them learn to think for themselves, as they strive to prevent free thought and action among the sheep, and enforce their will on the rest of the community.

For instance: conservative sheep refuse to allow two adults to marry or unite outside of the context of their man-made religious rules, because of their egocentric shortsightedness and their desire to control the lives of everyone. When they can enforce their ego-centric, religion-based, holier-than-thou mindset on the rest of the community, it allows them to further expand their influence and their selfish desire to play god and direct the course of people's lives rather than allow people freedom of choice, which scares the shepherds. Our ancestors came to America to get away from religious dictators and religious persecutions, to enjoy the life, liberty, and the pursuit of happiness that is guaranteed by the U.S. Constitution.

All of the organized religions are man-made. It is obvious by what they say and how they say it. They control the lives of their flocks, telling them what they can do and how to do it, and the flock is not aware that it is happening.

(Note to reader: If, as you are reading this, you are thinking, "Yeah, there are a lot of those cults and other weirdo groups out there...," but you never thought of your flock as being one of "those" and having such a controlling influence on your life. You go there because you want to; you enjoy going, and you love going, and you feel it is good for you, and would feel lost without it; blah, blah, blah, blah, blah. If so, then you need to take a long, hard, objective look at your religion. You may be more of a sheep than you realize!)

Try this: Skip church meetings and church relationships for the next month or so and see if you start to understand the world a bit differently. The constant brainwashing that has been a prominent part of your life will start to wear off, and you may actually experience your own thoughts about the Earth and the rest of the world around you, instead of what the flock and shepherd want you to experience. Soon you may realize that the universe does not rely on some god or any other imaginary figure, but it takes care of itself. Man is not in charge of the Earth, despite what you have been taught by your religion's shepherds. The

Earth is in control, and those who wish to live a long and peaceful life, should start paying attention to what it is teaching rather than the superstitious dinosaur dumplings that they have been swallowing since childhood. The man-made religions worship an imaginary god that hovers over the world watching everything and controlling everything because the god created it all. These gods are credited for all the good that happens, which is blindly accepted by all the faithful sheep, without a shred of proof or truth. But none of these all-powerful gods have ever prevented the harm caused by the Holocaust, wars, terrorism, natural disasters, tornadoes, hurricanes, floods, tsunamis, volcanic eruptions, earthquakes, and the Chicago Cubs losing streak, etc., because the man-made gods are impotent!!

Since gods do not participate in what goes on in this world, especially when there are really important needs for their omnipotent talents, then why worship them?

What good is a god that does nothing in the face of severe need? If all that these gods are good for is to be given credit by the flocks for everything that the Earth and the elements are doing naturally, then they are as false as those who promote them. When the Earth shrugs, all the prayers from all the faithful of all the religions are powerless to change the body count.

The universe is made up of the elements: air, fire, water, and earth. Many of the ancient cultures had a great respect for these elements as they knew that their lives depended upon them. Many cave paintings depict a respect and appreciation for the land, the air, the water, the trees, the animals, the sky, and fire. The ancient folks knew that their existence depended upon these things and they revered them. These elements are not man-made. They have been here since long before life ever started to breathe. Without them, there is no life and no Earth;

the central focus of the elements, where it all works in a harmonious, if sometimes cacophonous, symphony of life. If you must worship something, worship the Earth. It is truly worthy of respect and reverence.

Anyone raised as a member of any of the man-made religions from their birth, probably think that their view of the world is the only way of thinking about anything. But if they ever get the chance to avoid the weekly brain washing and start to think for themselves, they will find they can think more clearly. After a few weeks of thinking for themselves, without the automatic guidance that has been programmed into them from birth, they will start to see things differently. Be warned: you may be confronted by some of the other sheep or even the shepherd who will try to drag you back into the flock, because the rest of the sheep are afraid that the free one may be right and they are wrong, and they cannot deal with the insecurity of not having a shepherd tell them what to do or knowing that sheep got away and are learning to think for themselves. The story of the lost sheep demonstrates this: a free thinking non-sheep is willing to think outside the flock. In Matthew 18, 10 – 13, the shepherd is so concerned about the one sheep that has "gone astray" that he leaves the entire flock, because he knows they are well trained, and searches for the one until he finds it and puts it back with the flock, to maintain his sense of total control and self-satisfaction of having all of them under his control. This sounds like Paul giving orders to the new shepherds to prevent them from losing control of the sheep, which keeps the offerings coming in at the proper percentage.

The flock is mentally and emotionally fragile due to their dependence upon peer pressure and group mentality. Everyone strives to keep everyone else on their same level so they each feel comfortable knowing that no one else is any better off than they are. This 'flock mentality' is a resounding," No!" to any new ideas or progress of the simplest kind, and especially to one's sense of individuality. If it is not found in or supported by biblical verse or some doctrinal statement from the shepherds, it is rejected without any opportunity of review.

Though unsure of the author of this poem, it will be included here anyway, because it says it so well: (from the rock musical: "Tommy", written, scored and adapted by Pete Townshend 1975, music by the Who 1969).

"Of all the things in this world,
    to remove the veil from your eyes,
        nothing could be more simple.
When you get no answers,
    or real solutions and yet, no one has
        the guts to leave the temple."

Peer pressure keeps these religions functioning and as powerful as they are. The peer pressure makes the operation appear to self-promote its programs and popularity as if magically, by constantly pushing the idea that if you are one of the chosen, like sister-Bertha-better-than-you or any of the other holier-than-thou (s), then you are more godlike than regular people, and therefore a perfect example of how everyone else should be. This mind set is extremely appealing to most humans. It inflates the ego and strokes the super-ego, while tickling the Id often enough to keep a person off balance and in need of the comfort and salvation the religion provides. The religion creates both the problem and the solution, often in the same sermon. Once a free-thinking, rational person gets out from under the weight of the peer pressure and the feeling of obligation to the religion and the flock, by throwing off the shroud of guilt they have worn since childhood, they might actually experience true freedom of thought. The blinders will wear off and they will see truth much more and more clearly. The milli-micro-electrical circuits that allow their mind to think and process information will now be able to freely and clearly process some real information that has not been sifted and censored by the superfluous, superstitious, self-centered mind set of the flock. The same living spark that carries thought from neuron to neuron in the brain, will also inform and teach them about the world once they open their eyes and mind and remove the man-made wall that insulated them from truth and knowledge, which their religion and flock had enforced upon them since they were indoctrinated.

The sheep are afraid to turn from the pseudo-security of the notion that their next life will be better, which keeps them from making better use of this life, treating others better, and living in the real world. They keep listening to and trusting the egocentric shepherds that want only their money and care little about them or their neighbor except when they are in that pew and putting their hard-earned money in that plate that keeps coming and coming, and coming....

Where does all that money go...??? Who controls it once it enters the plate...???

Is the religion's building more like a magnificent palace, reflecting the shepherd's ego, who wears his robes of office like a king holding court...while he invests in hotels, owns large homes, planes, yachts, and drives a substantial auto?

Or does the organization actually use the funds to help those in need as it works out of a modest building, with a shepherd who actually ministers to the needy?

WHO IS BEING SERVED?

The poor who have no extra anything and yet their faith makes them feel guilty if they don't put something in that plate....

or

The fat cats like sister-Bertha-better-than-you or the other holier-than-thou types who drive up to the palace like they are royalty in their royal coaches, and put on a grand show of leading the faithful, with a potent pretense of phony philanthropy.

If their gods actually existed, wouldn't they reward truth and integrity and punish the lying hypocrites? Isn't that the message that is taught from the pulpit, week in and week out? When the sheep live their overt lives according to the morality preached by the shepherd, they all assume that everyone else is doing the same. The self-serving, hypocritical shepherds, appear to be a paragon of good, all the while they are shearing the sheep and taking advantage of the honest, hard-working, god-fearing members of the flocks. The ones who profess the loudest about being saved and having found the 'way' are usually the worst hypocrites, doing whatever they like to others in order to promote their own personal agenda and prosperity. They feel it is the way their god wants them to be.

Since the god does not participate in their life, why do sheep continue to participate in the flock? When they pray, they do not expect a real answer since they are so brain-washed to accept the explanation of the spin-speaking shepherds when they tell them that the answer was a bird singing in a tree or some other natural event, or that "sometimes the answer is no" Surprise! The shepherd does not care about the sheep, only the needs of the shepherd, often in the form of some new accommodation for the shepherds to use that's more elegant than it needs to be. The next time they ask for more money, tell them, "sometimes the answer is no", or that its invested in a college fund for the 'kids', so they can escape the flock mentality and learn to think.

When most flock members pray, they feel that the inner voice they hear is their god and they must follow whatever it tells them. That small voice that so many refer to as their god, is really just that persons ego expressing its desires as their mental process tries to sort out possible behavioral responses and pick one that best suits their self interest. Even the most brainwashed sheep still have mental capacity, but only within the parameters of the flock mentality. They have learned to praise and envy those who claim to have had direct contact with their god, and they are all so anxious to have such a crowning moment that they constantly refer to their normal mental process as a conversation with their god. They are so naive and so completely controlled by the flock mentality, and they are so enthusiastic about the notion of talking to their god, that they lose track of their real thinking ability and their thought process becomes stagnant in their effort to be good and faithful sheep.

Humans are mortal, but they desire immortality ever since the man-made religions have been giving them the false hope of achieving it after death, and the shepherds maintain the illusion in order to maintain their own comforts and status.

Man-made religions are established by insecure people who desperately desire to design the world in their own image, to be a 'somebody' with the ability to control the world around them. The same world in which they have felt so terribly alone and helpless for the vast majority of their miserable lives, becomes their personal goal: to be in charge of as much of it as possible. The problem arises when these insecure, emotionally immature, childlike people, who are mentally strong, but morally bankrupt and even depraved, somehow manage to insert themselves into a position of authority, usually by offering a childishly simple solution to the world's problems, and enough immature and naive people of average intelligence see them as their "savior"; the role they have sought for themselves their entire miserable life. The plot is set into motion and soon the entire world must deal with the new 'boss' of a large portion of the population. Take, as an example, the story from the Bible of how Saul of Tarsus became Paul and soon a large portion of the world was either embracing or fleeing from something called Christianity. Paul was a citizen of Rome and could not even do a good job of persecuting the remnant followers of the earlier prophet called Jesus. He figured out that he could go farther as their leader, since they had none, and it made a good story to add to the oral history about the prophet. The result was a well-paying gig for Paul for the rest of his life, playing the all-powerful demagogue over the naïve peasants of the then-civilized world. An amazing aspect of his life is that nothing is known or written about him until after he died, and then only in the Bible which was controlled by the church fathers of Rome. The Roman Empire was able to convert this influence into the Holy Roman Empire, which became the Roman Catholic Church and is one of the largest, most powerful financial corporations on the planet. Paul did get a sainthood out of it. Like all other man-made religions, the Roman Catholic Church would have everyone believe that they and their god have been around and in control of everything since before the Earth existed.

All of the man-made religions are similar in their total, superstitious commitment to an invisible, supernatural, personified deity that hovers above the Earth. They are operated as a business that produces no product in exchange for the tax-free cash contributions upon which they depend for their operational budget. The membership is like a flock of blindly ignorant sheep, led by a hierarchy of ego-driven shepherds, and required to follow ritualistic processes very specifically. The rituals have been so historically habituated into their lives that they are their way of life. Each religion is centered around sharing common spiritual experience of faith and obedience, guided by a written text, leading to redemption and some form of a life after physical death. This is the main selling point for most of them. There is usually one god, who is all-knowing, all-powerful, all-loving, all-forgiving, etc., but very stern about punishment, and extremely arbitrary. No one can ever know when or how or why the god does what he does, which keeps the god from being understandable, or predictable, requiring interpretation by the shepherds, and thereby giving lots of flexible leeway to the shepherds to interpret, in their own interest, the way and will of the god. They are more concerned with doing things certain ways than with thinking about why they do them at all. When they have done the rituals the same way as they have been doing them for over a thousand years, and they still get no results; why do they continue to do them?

All man-made religions include similar aspects in their organization, though some are more loosely structured than others. These defining aspects include but are not limited to;

1. A human-looking god, creator, their idea of the prime mover of all things.
2. A creation myth, how they would have done it, if they were god.
3. A creed : a summary of the basic superstitions.
4. A written text, considered sacred, because their god wrote it.
5. A pseudo-historic messenger, a behavioral example.

6. A hierarchy of priests, formal or not, shepherds for the sheep to follow.

7. Male dominance: testosterone-driven traditions.

8. Sacraments; the magic shows that help promote the mystery.

9. Symbols to remind the sheep and reinforce superstitions.

10. The financial focus, the real driving force.

11. A place to meet, to worship the god and leave the money.

12. A sense of community, enforced by peer pressure.

13. A liturgical calendar; orderly repetition enforces beliefs.

14. A self-promoting sense of believing; spinning myth into truth.

15. Good vs. Evil; keeps the soap opera alive.

16. Obedience, based on fear and peer pressure.

17. Experience. Repetition of superstition = perceived sense of "faith".

18. A sense of knowing: Repetition of myth = perceived "truth".

This writing has been set up as a process toward knowledge. The interrelatedness and importance of these aspects to the ongoing maintenance of the man-made religions, which is crucial to their survival, will unfold just ahead, followed by a section for those seeking a true sense of rational knowledge; a stepping stone for their path toward truth.

An ancient piece of wisdom from an anonymous writer:

"To each is given a bag of tools,
An hour glass, and a book of rules,
That each may build 'ere his work is done,
A stumbling block or a stepping stone."

May this be a stepping stone for your journey.

A God/Creator

The sheep spin their desires into reality in their mind.
Self-deception becomes the norm.

An ethereal being who was and is always there, and is
responsible for everything that exists and everything that happens
everywhere. The one that hovers over the world, lives in 'heaven'
and controls everything that happens to everyone, everywhere. It
was crucial to the early concept of the invisible god to place him
in a hovering position of control above the Earth so that no one
could challenge his existence since they could not reach it to
prove him not there, and since all the weather came from above,
it gave credence to the gods existence. Most people thought he
looked like a grandfather, until the rise of feminism, then it
became a bi-sexual or androgynous being, making it even harder
for some to relate. It is hard to give up the historically habituated
concept of the god who looks and acts like the ideal grandparent,
when, for centuries, most religions have had at their center a god
who was always portrayed as a perfect-in-every-way grandparent
who is always keeping an eye on everyone and watching over their

activities. The flock is encouraged to be awed by the super-ideal, mythically fantastic being who can help them solve their most severe problems (although he never ever really helps).This teaches and reinforces complacency so the sheep learn to expect no real answer to any of their prayers, and keeps some from ever facing and dealing with the reality around them and it can make them incapable of handling life, very sheep-like, dependent upon the flock for support rather than developing their own capabilities to deal with the real world, far too similar to a drug addict's dependence upon their fix in order to feel good and function like the robot they have become.

This 'god phenomena' has been so deeply imbedded in the minds of such a vast majority of the world's population for so many generations by virtue of the indoctrination methods that begin at infancy, and with the help of centuries of the religions' join-or-die methodology, that the concept is historically habituated into the mindset and is considered to be real true fact. It is a difficult myth to overcome except for those who can actually think outside of the flocks.

The early religions created the concept of the creator to help them cope with and explain the things about this planet that they never took the time to really understand. It has always been much easier to invent myths and superstitious rituals to cope with the world, since small minds cannot comprehend the vastness of the universe and how it developed through the natural processes of physics and chemistry. If all is controlled by the god, then the sheep can go happily through life without a care or responsibility for anything.

True intellectual growth is the enemy to man-made religions, who prefer that the flock remain ecstatically ignorant and mired in the depths of superstitious euphoria. The 'priestcraft' of shepherds keeps the flocks in the state of blissful ignorance in order for their corporations to continue and progress, so they can keep putting stickers in biology text books.

The problem surfaces periodically when a natural occurrence such as an earthquake, hurricane, or the largest-ever tsunami sweeps thru a section of the Earth and kills thousands, believers and non-believers alike; countless dead and missing simply wiped off the face of the Earth. When asked why such a thing could happen to so many people, the religion usually says, "the lord moves in mysterious ways", or "the ways of god are not known to man", because their god is totally helpless to either prevent, stop, or correct such a disaster. When the Earth shrugs, their god is nowhere to be found.

A better response would be to encourage people to understand that it is foolish to build your homes and businesses in the path of the natural elements, and if they do they must be responsible enough to learn the ways of the Earth so they can have some warning when the Earth is about to shrug, or accept the consequences without complaining. Since the earthquake areas and the hurricane prone areas are known, why are people foolishly building their homes there? Do they really believe the god will protect them?

Give the Earth and the elements the respect due them. They are in control. Not Man, and certainly not the impotent gods they invented.

Those in charge of the man-made religions prefer their god to be conveniently located and thereby controllable. They gave their god a personality; omnipotence, omniscience, complete immortality, and all possible abilities, then they gave their god a home; temple, church, synagogue, mosque, etc., and he can always be found there, because the religion makers say so. The buildings are revered and respected as having the same powers as the god, and, by association, so are the shepherds. Some flocks believe that their god is there whenever two or more of them are there, according to their text, (Mt. 18:19-20).

This gives man the ability to control the god, who, on the contrary, is supposedly in control of all things, and does what is best for his flocks. The contrariness continues when it comes to explaining why the god let thousands of people die in a hurricane, flood, volcanic eruption, tsunami, or the Holocaust, because "god moves in mysterious ways.... ways unknown to man". This is how sheep control their god by making excuses when their god never shows up at those moments. The sheep make excuses to maintain their man-made god as a god, thereby maintaining the phony façade of their man-made religion. They are also quick to point out all the impotent and impassive ways that their god is involved in the day-to-day operation of the world; like the 'miracle' of birth that is a most natural process that often requires no help at all, or someone overcoming cancer because they got mad enough to fight it, got stronger and won, or the miracle of Spring that comes every year, because these are obvious positives in the world and they want to be sure that their god gets credit for doing them, because their god really does nothing at all. The sheep would rather keep supporting the phoniness of their religion than give up the perceived sense of security. As phony as it is, they believe that it is all they have. The ignorant of the world will always believe in the illusions of the spin-speaking, scam artist, shepherds.

Many will hear truth but choose to not believe it because it is contrary to the historically habituated superstitions that have been so deeply imbedded and in control of their lives. The man-made religions have controlled the minds of the masses for hundreds of generations by the continuous reinforcement of the lies that keep the sheep from recognizing truth in front of their face.

The Earth developed over millennia by the principles of Physics and Chemistry. Those who refuse to understand the truth about the Earth will continue to plod along, believing all that their shepherds tell them without ever knowing the true state of knowing. They do not know; and they do not know that they do not know.

Creation

Ancient man drew from his own creative activities to explain how the world got here. Often a single culture had several creation stories, and in all cases their god is the creator. For example: the world was woven on a loom in Egypt and India; the Babylonian god 'Ea' wove reeds to cover the primeval waters and then covered it with earth; another Egyptian theory where the Earth was molded as a potter would shape a vessel; from the American Indian and Hebrew, once the Earth was there, the human is molded from clay; another from India had the Earth formed through sacrifice; or built it as a master craftsman; or spoke it into existence by a magical word or phrase (Israel, Babylonia, India, Egypt). The sexual union of the parent gods, heaven and earth, was a common motif in Japan, Egypt, Greece, India, China, and America. Many others started with the basic elements of air, fire, earth, and water and built a world from there.

In the Middle Ages the creation of the universe out of nothing became the established 'truth' for Judaism, Christianity and Islam. This was the time for a great deal of invented truths being established for the sheep by the shepherds.

In order to account for how everything came to be, it was

necessary to explain how their god created everything from the vast, formless, nothingness that was here first. These unnatural myths have little to do with facts. The magical explanation of how their god, who was not created but always was, decided to make a planet, stock it with life forms visible today, which did not develop over eons of time, but just happened : abracadabra….!!!!

To accept this, they must turn off their intellect and ignore all the archeological evidence and scientific discoveries which point to a gradual development of the planet and many species over a vast period of existence, unlike the creationists' version of a few thousands of years. The creationists have no sense of the nature of Earth or the elements, and make no accounting for the dinosaur bones or other forms of life that preceded the current era, or the other planets, and have a lot of other continuity gaps in their explanation of how this came to be. In some of the Bible-belt communities they even installed stickers in the high school biology books stating that evolution is only a theory. Not back in the 40's or 50's, but in the year 2000!! So where did all those huge bones come from? Bubba's backyard barbecue…??

The creator also told the first creatures to populate the world and have dominion over it. It would be contrary to this line of thought to practice birth control or to become sensitive to the needs of the Earth. Man is in charge. God said so. You can hear this every Sunday morning from all the conservative preachers along the Bible belt, or the crystal cathedrals, who live real well on what they say the lord provides for them from the TV ratings and the books and trinkets they sell, by scaring the sheep every week.

The religions also have a belief in the end of creation, their god's ultimate punishment for all the evil the sheep have done, but only applicable to those who have not been 'chosen' or 'saved'. This creates a strong urge among the naïve to become chosen or saved, and they fall deeper under the spell of the flock and the spin-speaking evangelists. The creators and supporters of this end-of-the-world myth, have a severe disciplinary agenda and vivid imaginations full of twisted thinking, designed to scare the flock into huddling closer under the blanket of the flock's salvation process. The same type of evil-guided mind is obvious among the priests-of-prey shepherds who contrive to abuse their position of trust to inflict their obscene desires on the innocent sheep of the flock.

During the middle of the 20th century, it was not uncommon to hear fundamentalist preachers proclaim that the end of the world was near and they would give the exact date and time they had calculated from various biblical passages that their god had directed them to read. They never took into account the fact that when the world switched from the Julian to the Gregorian Calendar starting in 1582 and onward, there were 10 – 11 days subtracted to bring it into planetary agreement, depending upon when each area switched. After their predictions failed to produce Armageddon, they were seldom heard from again. They probably spent the rest of their time putting stickers in biology books, so they could spend more time around the high schools.

Earth evolved over billions of years. It is in charge. We are just along for the ride.

Creed

A statement of what the religion believes, without question, to be their basic foundation principles, their theology, a summary of the superstitions that form their beliefs. It serves as a guide for the faithful, describing their invented deity and what they are supposed to believe about him.

The theology of the group is outlined by their creed, but it is usually quite confusing and even contradictory with a lot of spinning of the details, words and phrases. The statements which are not based on facts but on blind faith in mythical stories designed to provide proof of their religious doctrines, often require a spin doctor to unravel them. Theological enhancement involves further spinning of the superstitious inventions to make them more acceptable to the flocks, and having nothing to do with truth or reality.

Imagination + spin + agenda = religion.

It is the same as using one lie to explain another lie. The longer it is allowed to continue, the deeper the blanket of lies becomes, until it is so preposterous that everyone believes it to be the truth, and they are told it is the truth because "gods ways are not known to man". The shepherds use the god's "mysterious ways" to hide lies. Starting with the earliest theologians, who were anxious to save their lives and show support for the religion du jour that was killing non-believers. They spent their adult life spinning the invented facts into some form of understandable doctrine, as they tried to explain what previous generations of theologians invented as facts to support the biggest scam of all time: man-made religion.

Their theology is designed to be a crutch: something that the sheep are convinced that they cannot live without, and yet they are equally convinced that they are stronger because of it. To miss a flock meeting is like trying to take a step without the crutch that they are convinced they must have to avoid falling. The flock is repetitively indoctrinated, from their earliest year, that their god and messenger, as represented by the religion and the shepherds, must be the focus of their lives or they face the most horrible of deaths. They learn to fear god and the shepherd as well as the peer pressure of the flock. There is no questioning of the authority of the shepherd or the text, only listening and memorizing. Don't think about it, just learn it!!

The sheep believe all of the invented mythology and superstition under the headings of dogma, doctrine, and creed. The scam continues to abuse the faith and trust of the sheep who seek something to believe in but are given instead the self-promoting decrees and superstitious life plans of the man-made religions.

The invented concepts are designed to attract the naïve sheep to the grandiose words, elaborate trappings, magical deeds and mythical promises which amaze and confound those seeking something of value to believe in and follow. The only proof of these creeds and doctrines is what happens in the naïve minds of the flocks. When people want so desperately to belong to something powerful that they convince themselves that it is real and true, and from then on, the flock indoctrination and ritualistic reinforcement take over and they give up their freedom to become a member of a flock of sheep. Shepherds take great pride in boasting about how a child will be theirs forever if they have them for the first five years of their life...historical habituation. In historical perspective, creeds are handy summaries that were written to deal with religious situations, designed to speak to some urgent needs of the time in which they were written, and were used as tests to prove orthodoxy and the loyalty of the sheep. Because they are a written contrivance, they cannot be contemporary to any but those who wrote them, at the time they were written. Consequently, they are inadequate to deal with new developments and/or crises experienced by the sheep or the shepherds, in the centuries since they were written.

Everyone on this planet already belong to the most elite group known in the universe: inhabitants of Earth.... Earthlings. The only known planet that supports life, as we know it, so far. That is a very exclusive organization. The creed would be: Earth rules, because it does.

Written Text

Each man-made religion has a written guide which, in some cases, is believed to have been written by the hand of the god. The text is considered sacred and holy and sometimes is revered as much as the god. This serves as the handbook, providing guidance for the flock, and is often subjected to diverse interpretations. This text includes the rules, the do's and don'ts of the religion, and a great deal of what is accepted as the historical traditions of the religion. Before these ancient oral traditions were written, they were spread by word-of-mouth, so the original body of the material was exaggerated, twisted, forgotten, or just left out by bards. Similar to the folk lore of early America; the tall tales of Paul Bunyan, John Henry, Pecos Bill, Davy Crockett, and others were subjected to excessive exaggeration, twisting, and outright lying to make them more appealing to the audience, in just the past 200 years or so. Compare the stories about Jesus/Christ, Saul/Paul, Moses and the tablets, Mohammed, Joseph Smith and the golden plates, etc, to see the truth was either missing or stretched out of shape, and exaggeration was more present than not.

Most written historical documentation had dissolved into dust by 800, owing to the fragility of the parchment or papyrus medium on which they were written and the lack of suitable storage facilities. The only available written manuscripts were very fragile and costly, hand-written parchment rolls, even the writings of the religion scarcely survived. Most of what was later referred to as the historical documentation of the religion were bits and pieces that had been rewritten and rewritten, by hand, whenever the parchment became too fragile to handle, and much was originated by religion-authorized authors to represent the agenda of the religion in its mission to control the minds and spirits of the populace.

Before the printing press, (Gutenburg; circa 1450) the ancient text was handwritten, in very exaggerated style, and had to be copied by hand by lots of monks sitting for long hours at large desks. The inability to read probably prevented distractions. But the ability to copy accurately with good penmanship was a main requirement. The vulnerability to errors of omission or excess was certainly a large problem, begging the question: how accurate could any version of the text be? Can any human properly inscribe the words from their god without ever trying to promote a position that was dear to the writer or the one who was copying it?

"There was extensive use of hearsay, folklore, guess work and anecdote by the writers of the time, objectivity was not much of an issue. Even the scholars of the Middle ages were prone to see history as a journey of the god's children on their way to salvation." (J.W. Thompson, "A History of Historical Writing," Vol. I. New York,1942.)

Time reveals all things…that is, unless someone's ancestors burned the records. Papal appointed committees with subjective agendas, some of whom probably could not read, established standards by forbidding, censoring and even burning written texts, and some authors. Since the 1500's, the Roman church called the list of prohibited texts an 'Index' and included the names of authors, which was often a death warrant. This fit perfectly into the process which included the Inquisition, and gives new meaning to the term censorship, and involved a one-way visit into the Iron Maiden.

> Those who know not that they know not are shepherds
> of the sheep, who are kept blind to the truth.

The entire formative concept of the man-made religions is based upon a mythical, superstitious story that lost accuracy as it was expanded and exaggerated while it was passed down thru the years by oral tradition before it was finally written down, and then copied and copied by many who may have added or subtracted as they thought best. It is easy to see how a wandering story teller would enhance their stories to make them more appealing to the audience, or a copyist monk add his own opinions to sacred texts. But to represent as the gods truth; an exaggerated, twisted, manipulated, and spin-doctored version of undocumented fiction is simply to lie. The lie is self-perpetuating and has continued for centuries.

The Church of Rome has always declared that they are the true authority of Christianity and the Bible because they say they are the direct ancestor of Peter and the disciples, and they insist that since they were nearest to the actual events they are therefore the authority. This is of course confirmed by the Church of Rome and all the popes. There is no real proof of this.

The closest thing to a paper trail is by Catholic historians who have written that St. Cyprian, in the middle of the 3rd century claimed that Cornelius succeeded to "the place of Fabian which is the place of Peter" (from the Council at Ephesus, Ep. IV 8;

LIX,14). Tertullian wrote (about 220 AD) while disagreeing with the pope about absolution of sins, referring to the pope as the "Bishop of Bishops" … "who claims to have the same power to forgive sins as Peter had…" And, Hippolytus, during Pope Liberius(352 – 366 AD) the alleged author of the 'Liberian Catalog' of popes, "reckons Peter in the list of Roman Pontiffs" (Clement of Rome I, 259.) Certainly some very convincing facts???? But each pope confirms the lie and it becomes "truth" to the flocks.

Actual history shows that, until Constantine stopped persecuting and began tolerating the Christian cult in about 313, they were a serious threat and enemy to Rome. Since the Romans were the main persecutors of the early Christians for the first few hundred years, including the death of Peter, there is a real good chance that they also burned a lot of important documents, not the least of which could have been some of the earliest Bible scrolls. But no one can argue with a stone wall, especially once it has turned to marble.

The power-motivated fear in the minds of the leaders of the Holy Roman Empire and their offspring: the Roman Catholic Church, are responsible for the fact that very little contrary information is anywhere to be found because they burned what they could not understand, and anything or anyone that threatened them. But the lack of physical source is good proof that it did exist. They left history so one-sided, as though no other beliefs existed, that one must realize the lack of contrary information was deliberate. Simple diversity would have accounted for some alternative writings. The thoroughness of their censorship and editing points to the contrary writings that used to be in those gaps. Six hundred years of Inquisition can destroy a lot of truth.

The gaps in the written history were caused by their fires,

which were motivated by their fears. The same fears that they spread among their flocks, and caused so much history to be written in blood. Throughout history the Vatican has worked hard to protect its image as the holier-than-everyone-else epitome of holiness and sacred stuff in the entire world. But, by looking in the less obvious places, where they have left crumbs of reality, there can be found some of the truth that they have tried so hard to hide. Ex: Psalms, Song of Solomon.

Once the Roman Empire became the Holy Roman Empire led by the new Pauline Christianity, they became the standard bearer for the very cult they tried to eliminate by persecution; doing a total about face. They used the political advantages of the new discipline-laden religion concocted by them under the pseudonym 'Paul', and made it the way of life for the Roman populace. If anyone was not Christian, they were not allowed to live. The Holy Roman Empire spawned the Roman Catholic Church as its offspring, declaring themself to be the authority on all things relating to the god and all related texts.

Pope Leo XIII wrote an encyclical in 1893 declaring that the writers of the Bible were sacred and the Bible is not to be questioned. The Roman Church compiled and edited the Bible, by not allowing books and parts that disagreed with their agenda of controlling the population of the world, but they called it the "word of god". After they had destroyed some of it during the persecutions and took over the control of creating their authorized version, they declared themselves to be the official authority. Then, as the self-appointed authority, they gave their official approval to the text they compiled. That is not simply man-made, it is blatantly man-made.

Other fundamentalists are also very conservative in their approach to the text. They accept every word of it without question or critique, as if written by their god, as the infallible word of the god they worship. Many further believe that to memorize these words is to have their god inside of them, helping them stay on the straight and narrow path toward salvation.

The required memorization of vast quantities of text verses from the written text is crucial to the indoctrination and propaganda reinforcement process. Competitions with grand awards are held to further enhance the emphasis placed upon these highly valued achievements, often giving the flock work more emphasis than public school homework. Further emphasis comes from the fact that the parents are more in touch with and supportive of the flock homework, which never changes, than they are in touch with the public education homework which gets a bit harder each year to stay within current standards. The only time these sheep were in touch with a science text book was to put the stickers in them, warning readers that evolution is only a theory.

It is obvious which communities place more emphasis on the flock text than on the public education text because the education standards are often behind the rest of the country. And, by looking around the municipal buildings, town hall, schools etc, there is obvious evidence of the flock text such as a centrally located version of the Ten Commandments similar to what the past president of the NRA carried down from the mountain. With so much emphasis on text learning, the children have a hard time with conceptual aspects of public education because they have never had the chance to learn how to think. Most of what they have learned has been by rote memorization, and most of that has been what the flock has given them to learn. Their brains are not used to processing data and developing ideas so they never get a chance to grow up mentally and emotionally, just like their parents never did. It appears almost as though it is a genetic problem because the generations pass it on to the next generations. They continue to look at the world as a child does, and the flock mentality supports the process. The teenagers seek adulthood through sensory appeasement such as drinking alcohol, as well as sexual and other careless behaviors because they are forbidden to think outside of the 'flocks', they are frustrated by it, and they try to break away to find something that makes sense. But they have been raised on 'how to behave' and not taught how to think for themselves.

The Earth text is written in the rocks and layers of historical deposits that portray the record of all that has happened on the planet, and it is written in stone.

An Historic Messenger

Each religion has a quasi-historic human as a messenger from the god. Though not a real figure in any true historical records, they are given historical status by their subsequent followers, some of whom learned to write. The religion's own sacred text is often the only available "historical" record, which, if it has been around long enough, has become an accepted historic record by members of the religions who, by sheer numbers and historical habituation, have established each others written texts as 'historical records'.

Someone who was described as a corporeal person, able to walk and breathe and share the human experience, was the beginning of the entire process, and in some cases, wrote or participated in the text that started it all. Their appearance usually coincides with some volatile time in history when a major change is either about to or just did erupt onto their scene. The savior-guy steps forward during the turmoil and declares that he was given a solution by god, a solution that will bring peace and salvation to all who follow the teaching. He is the only person who knows what it is and he is sharing it with his growing group of followers who are all going to be sharing in the great salvation and peace.

("And if you drop what you are doing and come join us right now, we will include our version of the Bible, absolutely free!") Come on = con.

The Christians have Jesus Christ and Saul/Paul, who are more fiction and fantasy than fact. There is no written mention of them as real persons in any documentation of the era or the area. Some Roman documents mention a sect of religious zealots, though no names were recorded. Even the voluminous writings of the famous historian Josephus, who lived in the years just after the alleged death of Jesus, makes no mention of either "person" acclaimed by the Christians and the Bible as the most outstanding and influential persons that ever walked on the Earth. The Bible remains the only book that depicts Jesus and Paul as real people. Not surprisingly, the book that has been controlled and edited by the Church of Rome, the Vatican, the Holy Roman Empire, who use it to control the masses by maintaining the "cause".

If you look at it in terms of cause and effect; Jesus, the Christ, as invented by Paul, who was also invented, is the cause and Christianity is the effect. They must therefore go to whatever measures are needed to preserve the cause as real or they risk losing everything they have built over these past 1600+ years. The risk is so great that they have declared that it has "really" been 2000 years; dating Christianity to the alleged time of the birth of the alleged Jesus. They have the audacity to declare that the birth of their Jesus is when time began to be recorded, inventing credibility to go with the invented story.

Some of the similarities of the "historical" figures are interesting. At a time of great suffering and hardship, Moses, while leading the Jews out of Egypt, acquires some stone tablets inscribed by their god with the ten rules for life. Mohammed received revelations from his god in Medina in 622, which eventually became the Koran. Joseph Smith went a step or two further when he claimed to have been directed by visions to a hillside where he discovered golden plates covered with mysterious writing, which he was able to translate with supernatural help and it became the book of Mormon.

"Saul of Tarsus" writes that he had a revelation/conversion on the road to Damascus, changed his name to Paul, decided the world should do things his way, since he was getting nowhere in his persecution of the new cult. So he invented a religion using a few details about a popular prophet of an earlier age, related to a new cult movement, named Jesus. There had been rumors about the way the prophet disappeared from the area. Some say he had a better offer from a Buddhist group out East. Others said he had survived a Roman crucifixion, which enhanced the miraculous aspect. Paul claimed to be directly related to the followers of the prophet, Jesus, which would be hard to disprove in a primitive setting, and his alleged conversion convinced the naïve community. He went on to invent a spin-off version of the peaceful way of life preached by the prophet, and turned it into a fear-and-guilt driven religion whereby the disorganized community of dissenters were brought under the control of the Roman Empire. They became like sheep and would follow and swallow whatever they were told. He created a whole new religion based on his invented resurrection of the man called Jesus, attached it to the messianic beliefs of the age and soon had a well paying gig, selling salvation to anyone who would listen to him. So began the Pauline version of Christianity, based upon a struggle between good and evil to achieve eternal life, and which relies upon fear to keep the seekers returning for a salvation that really does not exist. By focusing upon the mythically superstitious part about the crucifixion/death/resurrection that cannot be proven and must be accepted on blind faith alone, the Church of Rome, then the Holy Roman Empire, created a flock of sheep addicted to the masochistic flip-flop routine of evil-pain-fear vs. grace-peace-salvation and they strong-armed it into a world-wide corporation of churches all passing their plates as much as possible.

Many make their business of delusions and false miracles, deceiving the naive sheep.

The same scam still reaps billions of dollars from the naive whose only problem is a weakness for things that sound too good to be true. The shepherds are scam artists who spin a sales pitch into a heavenly promise of eternal bliss, wearing custom-made clothes for their over-fed bodies, jewelry that rappers envy, manicured nails, expensive shoes and a well-styled comb-over that would withstand a tornado. They are prevalent on Sunday morning radio and television throughout America, especially the bible-belt. Some of the more brazenly arrogant claim they heal people in their magical, medicine/side-show style performance, during which they pass the plate (or buckets) a few times, and sell their tapes, books, and trinkets at the back door and on-line.

The exceptional few truly gifted philosopher/prophets spread calm in the face of fear, and peace in the face of violence. Men like Ghandi, the Dahli Lama, and the true Jesus. (Not Paul's invented man of smoke and mirrors.) They understood the elements, and their actions matched their words: peace at any cost. These were real messengers. They did not seek monetary gain.

Very little is known of others except thru the writings of their religion's text in which they are referred to as the son of the god or some such. When any of these messengers are not mentioned in the writings of the best known contemporary historians of the ancient world, it must be concluded that their real effect upon the known world was minimal at best. But through the promotion and publicity of the past centuries, some messengers have been made into sacred icons that cannot be dislodged from their position as sacred, holy, and chosen of god. They have become historically habituated into the world, and will stay there as long as the naive, lost, and lonely sheep seek comfort, peace, and salvation.

The simplest non-truth will grow, by repetition, exponentially, into an immovable, irrefutable fact.

Jesus taught, "Love one another," and, "Do unto others as you would have them do unto you". Paul twists and spins that into guilt, fear of evil, and dependency upon the religion for relief and salvation. Jesus taught that the Sabbath was made for Man, not Man for the Sabbath. Paul twists that into the opposite, wherein Man must serve the whims of the religion, the shepherds, and the pope. The religions have taught their flocks to fear and distrust others, and to be self-centered. Since the church depends upon the flock's dependence on the church, it must keep stroking their egos, teaching them self-satisfying behaviors and avoiding thought processes, keeping them flock-dependent, much like the doctors and drug companies reinforce dependency rather than healing.

Priestcraft

The person who well portrays all the virtues,
seldom has respect for any of them.

The most ego-centric of the sheep become shepherds, well-versed in the ways of the religion by attending institutions established by the religion for the purpose of creating shepherd pools from which they can continue to generate new flocks with shepherds that reinforce the historical habituation and maintain the continuity of the religion. Hiding behind a facade of the highest moral and ethical propriety, they are titled with a label of respect: priest, monk, pastor, rabbi, or such as fits the religion. They run the magic shows to maintain the superstitious control over the flock.

Ethan Allen in "Reason the Only Oracle of Man; Or, A Compendious System of Natural Religion" (1784), managed to strip away the contradictory and obscure of Christianity and rely on true reason as a guide to morality. He said that the churches used priestcraft (great word!) and witchcraft to hold people in ignorance for their own (the churches and the shepherds) selfish purposes.

They are specifically trained, designated, and set apart by special ceremonies to perform the sacramental rites by handling the sacred objects and saying the magic words which are designed to strengthen the controlling connection between the lives of the flock and the umbrella of control the religion maintains over the lives of its flock. They are set apart with such veneration that, too often, they become the focus of the worship, the star of the show, and develop a god-syndrome wherein they feel they are above all rules and laws and can do anything that they feel is right for them. Ask any former altar boys.

The religion encourages the flock to turn to the shepherd for guidance and counseling or to resolve issues. Members are to look to the superstitions for guidance rather than being encouraged to develop their human capabilities to think outside the flock mentality and be self-sufficient. Independent thought is poison to the flock mentality. Being a flock member of a man-made religion makes a normal human a dependent, brainwashed, robotic sheep following superstition spinners, who often think they are the god to be worshipped. As members become more dependent upon the shepherd to direct the worship, the shepherd becomes the star of the performance and the earthly stand-in for the god they are worshipping, often replacing the god in the minds of the flock, and in the ego-driven minds of the shepherds.

During the Second Council of Nicea in 787, they enacted disciplinary canons intended to raise the morality of the clergy, forbidding the selling of church offices, and forbidding sexually mixed monasteries. There must have been reasons for it.

Islam was invented without a shepherd/sheep hierarchy, more like an open dialectic style of honoring their god. The guidance was usurped by the more assertive to help guide those less capable. This permits numerous leaders to interpret the text according to their own personal agenda, allowing them to rise, by virtue of their ego-centricity and aggressiveness, to the top of the local political and religious levels, in their theocratic form of government. Ironically, this still creates sects and factions, like different flocks lead by shepherds, but with much less structure. The local warlord is also the local religious leader, like having the alderman also be the bishop

These spin-doctors are the enforcers of their god's will among the flock. The shepherds make decisions and take actions that the sheep follow and support without question. As this relationship is allowed to continue for years and years and spans generation after generation, the sheep become more and more complacent as the shepherds become more and more demanding, requiring blind obedience whereby the sheep simply do as they are told, as they pay for the entire process. The sheep are so far separated from the decision-making processes of the flocks that they are completely out of control and have no recourse but to go with the flow or stop participating, often by leaving the flock. But as flocks become larger and larger mega-conglomerates, it confuses and weakens the sheep's ability to function. Being so emotionally, mentally and even physically abused by the god-like shepherds who lead the flocks, the sheep blame their "lack of faith" for their inability to feel comfortable, and they accept the guilt and the penance as they struggle to belong to what appears to be a strong family of faith, but is in actuality a warped extension of the ego-driven shepherd's demented psyche. So the sheep put on a smiling facade and pretend to believe what they are told to believe, to maintain the status quo, and thereby maintain the superstitions and approve the methods used by the shepherds. The main goal of the shepherd is to maintain the flock's dependence upon the shepherd and maintain the complacency of the sheep.

Most shepherds believe they are in direct contact with their god, or they attach themselves to the papal infallibility doctrine, even the protestants, which leads to an even more inflated ego. The will they promote among the flock is their own, as the church becomes the 'altar ego' of the shepherd, wherein they become the absolute ruler of the flock and no one can challenge their authority or power.

Most have such an inflated opinion of themselves that they consider themselves to be above and beyond the rules that they enforce on the rest of the flock. They develop a strong sense of their own divinity that reinforces their arrogance and bravado and helps hide their guilt, especially from themselves, so they continue as if nothing is out of place as they float along, thinking they are above the rest of the human world. Some of the god-guys among us are just and honest men of integrity who perform their office with a stable sense of humility; whose only shortcoming is that they cannot get a real job and they use their abilities to support, defend and promote the man-made religions. They should not be confused with the evil, sick bastards who use their position to prey on the weakened and hurting, who come to them seeking consolation only to find fraud, abuse, molestation and rape.

The church had always been thought of as the safest of all places where children could play and study in complete safety, and young adults could find solace and comfort, until the threats no longer worked and the abused came forward to tell the dark tales of what goes on behind the ornate curtains. The ego-driven shepherds having their way with some sheep who could not protect themselves, was no longer the religion's dirty little secrets but became headlines, and it got deeper when the corporations knowingly participated by hiding the truth, protecting the molesters and abusers, by transferring them to another flock, and they continued with new, fresh victims. If the god was real, he would do a 'Sodom and Gomorrah' on some ancient cathedrals, and turn some shepherds into pillars of salt…hopefully, with a great deal of pain. It is hard to comprehend a god that would permit his representatives on Earth to be so foul and despicable…which further proves the non-existence of an all-powerful, all-knowing, all-everything god that cares about all of his creatures. Shepherds allow such weakness and cruelty among the leaders of their man-made religions because their standards are based on their own self-image, and therefore fraught with built-in frailties. Man created god in his own image, but their ego likes to say that god created man in his own image. The shepherds of the man-made religions are rarely of strong character and integrity. They act strong but are fraught with weaknesses which become all too obvious when they are raised to the position of shepherd and the absolute power given to them combine to corrupt them absolutely, in horrible ways.

Those shepherds who are unable to control their passions, claim to be guided by their god to justify their selfish deeds. Many even think that they are doing their god's work as they molest and abuse. They feel that their god provided the 'sacrificial lambs' for their use as a part of their god's plan, so they are never doing anything wrong. Their extensively brainwashed style of blind faith makes them feel that they are a special servant of their god and whatever they want is already approved by their god.

To focus on the Earth and meditate upon its power and wonder requires no middle man. The energy is always there within your mind like the radio sitting on the shelf; you only need to turn it on by tuning in to it and become aware of its power to calm and guide you. There is no magic, and nothing holy about it. It has always been there and you always have access to it. It will only happen when you are able to focus away from yourself and the selfish ways the man-made religions have been feeding you all your life, and toward the Earth.

Testosterone Traditions

All of them are male-dominated, allowing females only in subservient roles such as foot-washers, nuns, playthings, and such. This fact alone should be a major outrage against the man-made religions. There is no record of Jesus ever making a debasing reference to women, unless from a spin-doctored version from the poison pen of Paul, the Vatican-authorized authoritarian author according to the Holy Roman Empire and its offspring, the Roman Catholic Church. In spite of the lack of female influence or leadership in their religion, the impotent old men of Vatican-directed Christianity invented the concept of Mary as the "mother of god", (Council of Ephesus, 431 AD,) which may have had more to do with appealing to the pagans and their worship of the feminine earth deities, than with appeasing the female sheep, all the while not changing anything that would allow women any recognition or freedom to participate in the religion as something above the rank of servant. It is a cult which requires all members of upper ranks to have a penis.

The Mormons provide a good example of a very male-dominated society, where women have no voice at all and are expected to fulfill the wants and whims of their husband. The polygamous aspect is enough evidence all by itself.

The Muslims treat their women similarly. They are valued just above cattle, definitely second class status. Where the men are totally in charge and the women are subjected to many dehumanizing rules not the least of which is the wearing of the black robe and veil, and the men used to be polygamous.

The Hebrew tradition is so male-centered that it was forbidden for centuries for women to read, study, or even touch the 'holy' books. The male-domination continues along with the male-only text and all of the testosterone traditions

In the mid 1970's, the Presbyterians were showing their enlightened mindset by allowing women to have a "voice" in the religion's politics to the extent that they would have their own council in the pyramid structure of the hierarchy.

All existing councils were called the "council on...", and they were shortened to the anagram of their title; such the council on sacrament = COS ; until they ran into the Council on Women = COW!!!! The male hierarchy was not aware of any problem, for about a month until it hit the fan; the clamor could be heard for miles. It took a while, and a lot of committee meetings to arrive at a satisfactory label for that council.

For some really twisted gender invention, there is the Promise Keepers who claim to be putting men back in charge of things. But they do it by bullying and peer pressure at a stadium size pep rally. No women allowed. Put twenty thousand men in a stadium full of testosterone rhetoric, at $89. apiece, and what do you get? Over one million dollars in the hands of the organizers! Their message is: men can be suckered into most anything.

The few protestant religions that have opened the hierarchy to women, have limited their upward mobility.

Had women been more involved, they probably would not

have put up with the destruction of so much of the written history and documentation that has been burned by the church in the name of heresy. They would have insisted that every page and letter ever written, be tied with ribbon, into neat bundles and safely stored in cedar chests with sachet until it could be put on computer disc. Most of the sex scandals and controversies would not have happened because the historical arenas would have been cast with more hormonally-balanced groups of people, thereby avoiding a great deal of the stress and anxiety.

Being run at the top by a bunch of old, impotent men; the man-made religions express their ego needs through 'marking' and expansion of their territory.

The Earth-centered focus of the pagan way has always been and continues to be very maternal. Earth is like a mother to all who live here, the source of our being, a constant temperature below the frost line. Like a mother's womb at a constant survival temperature, insulated from the extremes, safe and comfortable. The man-made religions hated the pagans for worshipping the maternal aspects of nature. To the pagan, the female is to be honored and revered, not treated like some second-class property. The religions cannot begin to grasp the beauty, the peace and the intelligence of the pagan mind that still worships the Earth.

Sacraments

Special signifying actions mark certain moments of passage from one level of life to the next or certain occasions of special importance in the life of the flock member. These rites are designed to strengthen and reinforce the flocks feelings toward the church and toward the religion as a whole. These are symbolic actions which have become historically habituated into the lives of the flock. Great efforts are made to see that each and every tiny detail is practiced over and over and over until it becomes a well-ingrained habit, a cookie-cutter style performance that loses its meaning, overshadowed by the emphasis given to the behavior. The costumes of office, pontificalia, worn by those performing the rites, are elaborate and often lose function due to the excessive gold trim and overdone elegance, requiring the assistance of numerous altar boys to help them dress and undress.

Among Christians, when a child is born, they are baptized into the flock. About the time they start school, they have a first communion and start Sunday school. At about puberty, they are confirmed into full membership in the church, because they have an allowance or maybe a paper route or baby sitting income that they can put in the plate. When they get married, they have the priest perform the ceremony, adding a spouse's income to the plate. As the religious rules make them feel guilty and fearful, they can go to confession and be forgiven by doing some form of penance. As they approach death their fears and insecurities increase, they can purchase absolution, to guarantee their acceptance into heaven, or the relatives can purchase masses, or indulgences, to shorten the stay in purgatory, and hurry the dear departed towards heaven. Among these must be included the keeping of special days as holy days, requiring attendance at special services and events. For many, there are the very special sacred rituals called bingo or Las Vegas night.

Centuries ago it became common practice to convince the parents to protect the newborn infants from evil by performing a ritual that would mark the occasion and begin the child's relationship with the religion. The parents, being thoroughly indoctrinated and scared to do anything but what the shepherd requires, give over their infant child to be ritualistically washed in a ceremony of baptism to wash away the evil and obligate the parents to continue teaching the child the ways of the flock. The child has no choice in the matter since it is done to them before they can even talk, much less reason and arrive at a rational decision. The parents are acting out of their own uninformed notions of historically habituated, superstitious fears.

They install into their child their superstitious way of dealing with life, putting the child on the same superstitious path they have been on all of their life, giving the child no choice and no freedom. From that time onward, everything the child experiences will be filtered through the set of beliefs that the parents have installed into the child's mental hard drive as the default for all incoming data. The child will not be able to objectively experience the world around them. Instead of thinking how Socrates, Plato, or Pythagoras would approach a situation, they are trying to remember what Jesus would do, or how to avoid confession without getting caught. Their life becomes an imitating act, requiring no thought process, just memory. The only reason they have for doing something or turning away from something is that they are trying to do it the same way as Paul's version of Jesus would have done it, not a thinking reasoning approach to choices but an imitation of a person who is more myth than reality. They are not taught how to think, but how to imitate behaviors.

Their parents did it to them, just like the generations of parents before them. No one paused to ask why. It was always done this way and it will continue to be so because they have always done it that way. No one wants to upset the smooth flow of dinosaur dumplings and be cast out of the flock, since the flock has convinced all of them that inside is good and outside is bad. The superstition feeds itself by scaring them should they consider it, and making them feel guilty for even thinking about it. This is one thing that people will enlist their children into without the children agreeing to the idea, (and piano lessons). What compounds the problem is that it has become an historical habituation for each successive generation to do just as their parents did and keep the cycle going out of fear, peer pressure, guilt, or some combination of these. Continuous support of the superstitious, fantasy world pushes reality further and further away even though it is around them every day, and the paradoxical frustration makes the teenagers rebel. Their parents want them to grow up and learn to handle the real world, but their flock focal filter limits their scope to imitating the local version of adult behavior, because they do not know how to reason toward a decision, and, out of frustration, they seek to prove themselves by trying adult behaviors like alcohol, drugs, sex, and their car accelerator. Quite often, in the more fundamentalist communities, there is a large element of adults who have never grown beyond that teenage mentality because they were forbidden to think as real adults in a real world. Their idea of adult is alcohol, drugs, sex, fast driving, watching college or pro sports and trying to relive their experience of high school athletics. They have the number of their favorite pro race car driver on their car and their jacket...an overt expression of their need to belong to and identify with something meaningful to them.

The focus and meditation upon the Earth requires no such sacraments, processionals, special rites to be repeated and repeated ad nauseam. Once you have found the focus on the energy source, the doing of your meditation will be the only thing you will need and want to do. Sharing the knowledge with others and initiating open and honest dialogues about truth and reality will become a way of expressing your newfound life.

Symbols

Since most of the essential things of a religion are unseen, each has an historically established set of symbols, dramas, and myths to enhance the experience. During the earliest times, when few could read or write, symbols and oral traditions were the main form of communication. Symbols help to communicate and interpret the various expressions. Dramas help to show the flock how to act and behave, and express the various emotions, and show how they were supposed to impact human history. Myth-filled legends and traditions, usually exaggerated, further enhance the vividness of the religious experience, all creating more false credibility by reinforcing an emotional connection, requiring certain actions rather than any thought process.

False prophets, portraying charity and devout worship,
cloud the minds of the sheep with music and rituals
as they are sheared.

Members of the flock have learned to find a sense of comfort by repeating memorized prayers, phrases, songs, or such, as they hold certain symbols: cross, rosary, etc., or make certain signs;

crossing themselves, raising their hands over their head, kneeling, prostrating, etc, or perform special acts or behaviors supposed to bring forgiveness or relieve guilt, such as climbing a stairway in the Vatican on one's knees, making a pilgrimage to Mecca, or to Jerusalem to walk the same route that Jesus allegedly walked on his way to be crucified.

The sheep have been programmed to believe in the power of symbols making them cling to theirs and be fearful in their rejection of others. A Christian will become quietly pious in the presence of a cross or the Bible or a photo of a saint or 'Christ', and exhibit fear and trembling in the presence of a pentagram or some similar pagan symbol. They believe these man-made things have power to affect their lives, like a child afraid of the dark or ghosts.

A particularly interesting 'symbol' or 'gift' is seen among the very conservative, fundamentalist flocks, called "speaking in tongues", wherein a member of the flock starts jabbering incoherently in what they immediately identify as some sort of "sacred" language, which no one comprehends. They assume the person has been "chosen" by their god, and they are told to accept it as their god coming into their presence, or a miracle, or a divine message. The main drawback is that no one understands the words, but it is a great way to disrupt a boring sermon, and steal the fire from the preacher for a while.

Throughout the centuries these symbolic rituals have done so much to promote the mythically mysterious and superstitious aspects of their religions that the members of these flocks have come to think of them as reality. Like a child who is afraid of the dark but feels safe when they are holding their doll or teddy-bear, Christians are taught to approach their religion like a child, "for to such belongs the kingdom of God." (Mark 10:14) It is through these mindless rituals that the shepherds maintain control and superiority over the flock. Enforcing the practice of the rituals the flock must perform properly to resolve their fears and guilt towards their god, gives the flock a false sense of control over their lives when actually it is the religion that is in control of their lives, and their wallets. The flocks accept these routines without question because they are so historically habituated into their lives and a part of the flocks' communal and corporate personality. The constant struggle to maintain the minutia of ritual details keeps the flocks' minds too busy to think any individual thoughts.

The Roman Catholic Church is well-known for its emphasis on symbols and idolatry. Every couple of centuries a pope adds something new to the mix and it is to be understood as god's law. They believe if it came from the pope it is from the mouth of god. For instance, the Council of Ephesus, 431 AD, decreed the flock was to honor the mother of Jesus as a sacred aspect of the whole package, and by the sixth century, that she was assumed bodily into heaven, then the Dogma of Immaculate Conception in 1854, and after the pope was declared to be infallible in 1870, they really started inventing decrees, dogma, and the aptly named; papal bull. By 1950, Pius XII issued a papal bull wherein he defined the concept of the bodily assumption of Mary into heaven as a dogma, essential to the salvation of all of the flock, and it all goes so far as to present her as the one intercessor who could 'command' Christ, as if the immaculate conception invention, started back in 1263, was not enough stretching of the already pretentious 'reality'. More recently, Pope Benedict XVI, elected in 2005 following the death of Pope John Paul II, decided to forego the established requirements for bestowing Sainthood on John Paul II and started the process within a month of his death while the Catholic community was still emotionally connected to the loss and memory of one of the longest serving popes. The Church of Rome is hoping to regain some of the popularity it has lost over the past decades by milking this process for all its worth, and getting as much publicity as it can by establishing a new saint, that people remember as both a symbol and an idol, before the crowd has a chance to calm down and return to their routines. Good marketing, Benny.

The main symbol for any man-made religion is $.

The shepherds and the religions are guided more by money than by anything else. For centuries the religions have served god and mammon, in spite of what its written words direct. After all, the religion created the god so they could reap the mammon from the flocks.

The Earth has so many aspects that symbols are superfluous. You can not look at any natural part of the Earth without it guiding your thoughts to the Earth energy, once you have found your focus. Anything that is man-made is subject to the energies of the Earth. Earth needs no money. It continues to survive, alter its appearance, and maintain a life-supporting environment in spite of man's selfish attempts to control and abuse it.

Financial

In ancient times, offerings were pure animals to be sacrificed. Then Rome and other major centers started minting coins for commerce and 'cash' worked its way up to offering status, late in the first century AD., and the mission of the religions became:

Fear + comfort + guilt + salvation =
tax-free cash in the shepherd's coffers.

This is why and how the organization exists. If it were not financially fluid, mostly cash, and tax-free, it would not be able to continue. The tax-free status is protected by the sheep who are in the U. S. congress and use their flock mentality to maintain the tax laws, which helps assuage their guilt/fear that the shepherds maintain in them.

The faithful are encouraged to give money to the regular and on-going mission of the religion, which is to make as much money as possible. Some don't just encourage, they actually tell the members how much they will be donating during the next year. The passing of the plate is a regular part of most every meeting. Even if members mail in their check, the plate is still passed. If the entire format of the worship service were changed, there would still be a 'plate passing' to shear the flock. The term 'flock' seems so appropriate for those who go to be fleeced. They support a business that produces no product, just words of comfort to offset the words of discomfort which they also produce.

How much do you pay your shepherd for your salvation fix?

The man-made, false-security-blanket religion must maintain the illusion of reality in order to maintain the real reality of the incoming cash flow so they can build more and larger monuments to their egos, thereby providing job security for themselves and all the rest of the shepherds who cannot get a real job, and must hide behind the fancy, draped walls of their cathedrals with their elegant robes of office, and degrees conferred upon them by their own institutions. The cycle continues, the cathedrals get bigger, the robes get more elaborate, and the brains of the flock get softer as they bear the financial burden of the whole fabricated soap opera. All the while the shepherds keep shoveling their dinosaur dumplings, full of superstition and outright lies, as they go on about their business of putting stickers in biology books.

Tent revival meetings used to pass a basket (it holds more) every time the sheep got moved to stand and say, "Amen", often, a few times an hour.

The Roman church has a long history of selling things. The top of the list has to be indulgences; the invention whereby the relatives of the departed are able to shorten or eliminate the length of time the departed soul has to spend in purgatory before continuing its journey to heaven. Begun in the 3rd century and expanded during the Crusades,1095 thru about 1390's, when crusaders were granted relief from penalties built up while temporally sinning, and made famous when Luther kicked off the Reformation by nailing a list of the church's shortcomings to the cathedral door on October 31, 1517, probably while trick-or-treating. About 1567, most of these abuses ended when Pius V ended the practice of selling commissions to 'Pardoners', who sold our ancestors their way out of purgatory. Now the practice is in the form of masses that help the departed on their journey towards heaven, available thru donations of specified amounts.

A good example of the historical emphasis on money and its abuse surfaced when the throne of the Roman church was temporarily at Avignon, France, from 1309 to1377. Those seven pontiffs during the 66 years developed processes which would derive income through ecclesiastical appointments being bestowed upon the most worthy (translated : wealthy) office seekers who had their own agendas, leading to influence-peddling, bribery, and selling the same office to numerous people. This allowed the office-holders to wear the fancy robes and funny hats and be bowed to as they rode around in their chauffeured ox-carts.

A more recent example of the church's emphasis on money appeared in the news on March 12, 2000. A nun was being made into a saint by the Vatican. She had once been a wealthy socialite from Philadelphia, but she gave all of her $ 20 million to start an order of nuns to work with poor Blacks and American Indians. Certainly a most noble gesture, even if none of those minorities ever saw any of the $ 20 million. But since a requirement for sainthood is having performed a miracle, the Vatican, in its corporate wisdom, "discovered" that the millionairess-turned-nun was somehow responsible for curing the deafness of a 4 year old girl. Truly a miracle! But not as much of a miracle as a rich 30 year old giving twenty million to the church, becoming a nun, and ending up a saint. Now it is known what it costs to be declared a saint by the Vatican. This will serve as a suggestion to other millionaires as a way they can make a donation to the church in exchange for some similar recognition. Every time the church declares sacred status for something that is common, it demeans the power of the status as well as the authority of the church. It becomes more like in a game of checkers, where, just by crossing the board a man becomes a king.

Once the shepherds have the sheep convinced that they cannot live or function without the flock, the dependency becomes established. The sheep are securely 'flocked', and the regular fleecings or shearings continue. The fleecings are never too large to make the sheep uncomfortable, just large enough to make the shepherds comfortable and give the appearance of peace and unity. The shepherds preach and reinforce that, "money is the root of all evil", and yet they convince the sheep to bring and 'donate' as much as they can, so the shepherds can roll in it if they so desire.

The sheep are lead to believe that money is used for the god's work. How much money does a myth need to subsist? Actually, quite a lot. It is very expensive to maintain a superstitious illusion. The requirement of money further proves the man-made religions are man-made. Man requires money to feed his ego.

The Earth makes no such requirement. It needs no thing made by man.

A Worship Place

From the grand spectacle of the ancient palaces of Rome to the small, one room, frame building of the rural farm communities, each is special and sacred to its flock. Some, like the crystal cathedrals and other such seen in the weekly televised broadcasts, have been designed so elegantly that they draw the focus away from the purpose for which they were supposedly built. They have become an expression of the 'altar ego' of the shepherd.

The building is filled with symbols and is often a symbol in and of itself, in the shape of a cross, or some other ancient icon. For religions that claim to not believe in idols, there are an awful lot of statues and pictures; usually explained as serving as reminders of people and events. So, why are people kneeling and praying in front of it, and lighting candles at that particular place? Some churches have lots of different altars throughout the building, along with extra collection boxes for various reasons. There are often special, off-limits areas, behind elegant drapes, where the sheep cannot enter. Priests and altar boys only! This helped protect their outrageous secrets.

Ancient Hebrew temples had the section for the Holy of

Holies where only a certain priest may go and only on certain times of certain days.

The buildings are places for the sheep to gather to be fleeced/ sheared.

Too often, the building is thought to be sacred, a notion the shepherds encourage to reinforce their own holiness by association.

Earth is a place of worship.

A Community

These religions are defined by their community of faithful, the flock, who meet regularly and repeatedly, to get their dose of reinforcement of the religious experience. This reinforcement fix is crucial to the continuity of the religion, just as the next fix is crucial to the continuity of the habit of the drug addict, who would do most anything to avoid missing that next fix. Most sheep are so indoctrinated/addicted that they never miss any flock meetings/ fixes.

Questioning the belief system; what the shepherds define and the flocks defend as the truth, causes the group to bring pressure upon the questioner until they stop asking or leave the group, but since humans like to be a part of a group, this allows peer pressure to hold the group together, making it all appear to be a voluntary group of happy, contented, (though sometimes frustrated) sheep. The level of naivety among the flocks' believers is amazingly similar. Many well-educated people have a blindingly strong addiction to this type of community of faith. Most of the followers of the infamous Reverend Jim Jones paid with their life for such a naive sense of blind faith.

The community identity is enhanced by the particular way

they express the practice of their rituals and worship methods. Each sheep had to go thru the same initiation ritual after meeting and completing the requirements for membership and giving a portion of their life and income over to the religion, making the community a part of their personal identity. Membership in such a community does not add as much to the person as it takes from the person to add to the flock, turning the person into a well-rehearsed robotic, no longer able to think for themselves, a member of the flock, part of the flock identity and mentality, relying on the shepherds for decisions. A new member soon finds a way they can apply their talent to enhance the flock, whether it is singing in the choir or playing an instrument, reading to children, nursery-sitting, cooking, typing, or even as a handyman. They find a way to fit into the operation and become a useful cog in the corporate wheel, which allows the church to redirect more of their tax-free money to spend on expanding the operation.

The shepherds encourage peer pressure and indoctrination in the form of group gatherings, often disguised as social functions such as text studies, teas, youth groups and even sports teams. The more diverse the functions of these groups, the better the chance of having something that will appeal to any member or potential member of the flock. The broader the appeal the better the tax-free cash flow in the plates. Trying to become something for everyone causes the expansion of the flock, the need for larger offering plates, and a more corporate style of operation which increases the influence the church has upon more and more of the community. Soon it is influencing political policies, and politicians are addressing the flocks from the pulpits. Whatever happened to the separation of church and state?

For many, a main part of the community identity is centered on a shared belief in the personal salvation of each member of the flock. The concept of being saved or chosen requires no proof, since none exists, only a convincing performance of the concept by the member. The concept is very ego-driven, and easy for anyone who can act. When you hear 'conversion', think coercion. The concept of being 'chosen' allows the chosen one to become a cog in the flock mechanism, like a big fish in a small pond. These actors help maintain the continuity and a superfluous sense of 'the divine presence' among the flock. They assume that everything they say or do is approved by their god, therefore they can do no wrong. They often develop very unrealistic attitudes and expectations as their ego goes into overdrive and they develop an 'altar ego'. There exist many such congregations full of such altar egos, who so strongly identify with their god or the messenger that they feel they have a direct connection with their god's mind so they are not only chosen, but they become a chooser, passing judgment on those around them.

Often the community identity takes the form of an adolescent secret club with secret signals, greetings, and a team attitude that becomes competitive with other religious groups. It combines the holier-than-thou attitude with the my-god-can-lick-your-god mentality, demonstrating the naive ignorance that is so prevalent in the man-made religions. They become an exclusive club whose proclaimed mission is to reach out and bring in all who seek the peace and salvation of their god. (Read this last sentence again, slowly, so as to not miss that irony). Actually they seek and select those whose attitude and social status closely reflect their own as they seek more pockets to help fill the plates.

Anyone who loves true freedom will not allow a religion to control their life or tell them how to think. Most flock members feel they are thinking freely as they follow blindly along the same deep rutted path with all the other sheep. Their brainwashing was started so early and has been so subtle that they are not even aware of it happening. Their indoctrination began when their grandparents first joined as infants, as did the entire family, all of whom are unaware that peer pressure is a crucial part of the reinforcement and programming process that helps maintain their attitude toward the flock. If a teenager decides they want to stop going to church, the rest of the family gets on their case until they either cooperate or move out of the house. When sheep are deeply faithful and committed to their religion, the religion is actually controlling most of their life, and they are not free. They are dependent on the crutch upon which they lean for their emotional support. The more they rely on it, the more they need to rely on it. They become intellectually controlled, emotionally dependant, and eventually shut off their own ability to think and decide for themselves. Since religions infect mankind with false hope and unfulfilled promises that require them to die to find out that the truth is not as they were led to believe, there are no dissatisfied sheep who can report the true facts to the flock. If they rely upon their religion for emotional calm and peace of mind, they are not free. They are part of and dependent upon their community of faith; a very powerful and addictive crutch that is not under their control. They are complacent members of a flock. Let the congregation say amen…. "Baa-aa-aah!"

All of us are already members of the Earth community.

Calendar

Based on their historical record, often very loosely, there are set dates or periods of time during the year when certain activities take place, or a special celebration or remembrance is reenacted. These reenactments are a strong and required reinforcement of the fix for the flock. Many of these are based in the ancient understandings of the seasons, centered around the phases of the moon or the Earth's relationship to the Sun because those were the most important times of year to the earliest inhabitants of this planet. They had figured out that the days were longer and shorter at various times, and that this phenomena repeated in cycles, and they figured out the best times to plant and harvest crops, giving them reasons to celebrate. They found the shorter days lead to longer darkness and the need to put food away and find shelter from the cold, and they looked forward to the time when the days got longer and warmer, and that became the beginning of their life cycles, a good reason to celebrate. The real reason for the season was the Winter Solstice, Yule time.

As religion developed, the shepherds blended their superstitions with those seasonal activities of the pagans, who were soon-to-become sheep, to further cement the relationship.

Christians continued the practice of a day of worship every week, began by Judaism. They chose Sunday because the Jews had already taken Saturday as their Sabbath, and because it was easier to get a tee time on Saturday, when all the Jews were at synagogue. Sunday was named for the Sun god from pagan times, but some things were used to establish continuity with the pagans. Sun god—son of god.... Sunday; close enough.

Passover was already well established as a special time, so the Christian flock just adapted it to the celebration of new Spring outfits, purchased from the Jewish shopkeepers, and they called it Easter, named for the pagan Spring Goddess: Eastre. Eggs and bunnies were pagan symbols of fertility. Paul probably had a lot of issues around Easter time, so he twisted the pagan fertility rites of Spring into a somber and sober, execution, mourning and resurrection, taking all the fun out of Spring. No more bacchanalias.

Speaking of parties, the original Yule time was a celebration of the end of the darkest days, at the Winter Solstice when the Sun started providing more daylight. The Yule celebration was a rowdy and festive time, rooted in ancient paganism. The early Christian religion installed Christmas on the Winter Solstice of the northern hemisphere, making the birth of their savior coincide with the prehistoric, pagan celebration of the rebirth of the Sun, the actual beginning of longer days. It was easy to spin one into the other among the naive of the day, and it becomes even easier to maintain the current story since it has become historically habituated into the minds of the flock. This confirms proof that Christianity was man-made by someone in the northern hemisphere, and points out the weakness of such an invention. If it were created by a god that created the universe, then it would not be limited by such a human frailty as seasonal changes. Earth is not controlled by seasons. Seasons are controlled by the Earth.

The Winter version of the new clothes celebration is Christmas. Ironically, many have a Christmas Eve candlelight service where the dim light does not show off new outfits very well, and may even inflame a new hat. Since Easter and Christmas, the two biggest of the main celebration days, were too happy, making the flock too comfortable, the religion installed in front of each of them a multi-week long period for being uncomfortable: Lent and Advent. During these times the flocks are subjected to as much guilt and fear-mongering as can be wedged into midweek meetings, just as the holiday approaches and schedules are already pretty full. Paul would have been proud.

The religions calendar is quite adept at requiring attendance at extra services during these weeks, so the church can fill the pews and pass the plate during the week as well as on the weekends. Not unlike the greeting card industry, the man-made religions are always pleased for another special occasion. Mother's day and Father's day have become special occasions for the church, and there has been rumor (probably started by greeting card companies) to institute special days for the grandparents. There is already a day for the blessing of the pets, related to a saint that may have started the SPCA. The Church of Rome has a day for every saint they ever created, covering most of the year, causing those named after a saint to feel obligated to go to and leave money at a church.

Kwanza, one of the celebrations of one of the newer man-made religions chose as its time of celebration the period starting after Christmas; giving them a piggy-back ride of paid holidays, along with Hanukkah. It does tend to crowd the calendar at the end of the year, but makes for great press coverage, and gives all of them extra holiday time off from work. Had they chosen a non-holiday time of the year, they would have missed the extra days off. Is it a coincidence that their candelabra looks so much like the Hebrew menorah?

The Summer celebration of new clothes is called Mother's Day, and the church picnic usually comes near Father's Day.

The Earth calendar is all around us, once we learn to read and understand the seasons and the cycles in Earth terms. Earth dictates the calendar, we live by it. The reason for the seasons are the seasons themselves.

Believing

Members of the community of faith, the sheep, believe everything that their religion has taught them since they were initiated into the community as infants. Their parents did it to them because their grandparents did it to the parents, because their parents did it to them and so on back thru the generations. They have been part of the flock since before they could even understand what it was about. They and their family have always been sheep of the flock for as long back as they can recall. They have never been outside of the flock. It has always been a main part of their life. Their entire life has been translated to them through the belief system of the religion as members of the flock. They are historically habituated into the religion's set of beliefs. They have never really experienced the real world that they live in because they live in the state of being saved or chosen, which forces them to see with blinders on, hear through filters, and learn and understand through thick layers of historically habituated superstition. Being in the state of 'chosen' or 'saved' causes them to act as though they are better than and above everyone else. They have little tolerance for anyone who believes differently than they do, except as someone upon whom they may impose their belief system and try to convert them to their 'right' path.

The situation is compounded when they become so stubborn about their religion being the only true religion, that they are willing to defend it against all other religions, even to the extent of killing the 'infidels' to cleanse the Earth of such terrible plagues of ignorance, not realizing that they are one of the main plagues of ignorance that threaten the Earth.

Think of life as a card game. Seated around the table, each player represents a different religion. Each of them is so arrogant and self-centered that they will only play using their deck of cards and they do not allow the others to use their own cards because they do not like the colors or designs on the others' decks of cards. The hostility is such that the game is never allowed to begin and some would even kill another player to prevent the use of his cards because they are different from their cards. They only play with their cards and with themselves. Their idea of life is a game of solitaire, within the flock.

The man-made religions stifle knowledge and encourage blissful ignorance. The human mind seeks to know and understand unless it is so buried in layers of mindless superstition and habituated ritual that makes mountains out of minutia and turns the mind's focus inward toward self-serving egotism, ignoring world view in favor of self-view. The world no longer holds any real meaning for these sheep, whose main concern is for their own well-being. They want to save their 'soul' even though they have no real concept of what that means except in terms of the superstition-laden, smoke-and-mirrors, load of dinosaur dumplings that they gobble down every time they meet with the rest of the sheep. They all say they believe in it because everyone else says they believe in it, and the peer pressure of the flock creates and maintains a group mentality which then supports and maintains the superstitions as their own sense of reality. All the myth and superstitious fantasy that the man made religions are built upon give it the strength of a house of cards, and they all know it (down deep inside) but will never admit it. They will defend to the death the fantasy foundation they stand upon because it feeds their egos. As long as the brainwashing and regular reinforcement continues like a drug addict that has no fear of having to go thru withdrawal, and the organization maintains a self-feeding and self-sustaining mechanism of ego-driven sheep and shepherds who are without responsibility as they are told what to do and when and how to do it; the fantasy will continue. This is the flock mentality: keeping up with the joneses…. the Reverend Jim Jones!!

They wear a facade of pretense and phoniness usually combined with false bravado as they try to bluff their way through situations by quoting text passages. They have never experienced the real world or their real self. Their main goal in life is centered on going to heaven after death, after spending their life as a complacent, robotic sheep.

What Christians believe, they accept as true. Their only proof being the creative writings of the man-made 'Paul' and everything that the Roman Empire and the Roman Catholic Church invented. They believe that Paul's Jesus, their messenger, is the son of their god; that he was conceived in the womb of a virgin without the human process of intercourse. He was born as a normal human, and performed a lot of miracles before his death. He fulfilled all of the prophesied requirements for being the long-awaited 'savior/messiah' and as such, he died for the sins of the world, redeeming them from suffering. After he died from crucifixion (emphasis on fiction), he rose from being dead, allegedly proving resurrection/salvation, he went to heaven to live with god, and he still performs miracles. The only written record of these events is the Bible, and the sections narrating these stories were written long after the events were to have taken place.

Truth and reality inform us that these events are fiction, written to promote the political agenda of the writer (s). Just by writing it as though it were true, does not make it truth. Intelligent minds using reason and rational thought will have trouble accepting such man-made mythology. Using the Bible to validate stories from the Bible is like someone looking in a mirror to prove their identity by saying, "Yup, that's me."

Most believers want to believe because they are afraid to not believe. They have been conditioned to avoid the concept of remaining dead after they die, and to embrace the myth of being raised into eternal life, sitting in heaven with god as if they are going to become gods, which is a much more ego-satisfying concept than taking an eternal dirt nap and being worm food.

Members of these flocks believe and depend blindly upon what the shepherds tell them, which reinforces the role of the priest as god's representative, and discourages questioning the truth or validity of the religion. They act like well-behaved children maintaining the fantasy, the illusion of reality. Looking at the world as a child, is like looking through colored or smoky glass. Things are as they want them to be: a fantasy. An adult should see clearly, no longer thinking and acting like a child, but the religions keep promoting the same sort of naive fantasy world in order to maintain their control and keep the flock from seeing the reality around them with clear eyes and mind. They must avoid anyone who may rock the paper boat, because it cannot hold up to real scrutiny. It is a child-like fantasy world, but as long as everyone agrees it is real, because peer pressure keeps them afraid to not agree, the illusion continues as it has for so many generations.

The man-made religions help promote "welfare" mentality by becoming a crutch that the flocks cannot be without for fear of being 'cast out' and left alone. The shepherds reinforce the superstitious beliefs that form their foundation and keep the sheep blissfully unaware that there is a whole world of knowledge and wisdom outside the flock that would help and encourage the sheep to become real people: thinking, rational, and not just less fearful of the unknown, but willing to explore and embrace it in pursuit of knowledge and understanding.

Since the sheep have had their decisions made for them for their entire lives, it makes them very vulnerable to being controlled. The sheep become lazier and lazier and are grateful for it. They no longer have to generate any mental and very little physical energy. It has done for them so much for so long that they can no longer function in any other environment. The addicted sheep become dependent upon the flock and cannot break away, and worse, they do not want to, and they will defend the flock to avoid separation. The complacency is a downward spiral towards a weaker, dumber, sicker, and less intelligent society, and is already happening in America.

A good example of the 'dumbing down' of America is the "No Child Left Behind" legislation, which lowered the national education standards to enable those sheep in the welfare system of the country to be able to pass the minimum standards and get into college. This weakens the entire country!

The true believers of the man-made religions are among the worst polluters of the environment and the eco-system, because, according to their sacred writings, they believe that they were given dominion over the world to use however they please. They know little about the elements except, naively, as parts of the world. They blame the evil in the world or gods "mysterious ways" for the earthquakes and other natural phenomena that kill people. They have not learned to respect and honor the Earth and the elements.

The Earth does not require you to understand its seasons and cycles. But if you truly want to be a part of something amazingly awesome, you should learn the ways of the Earth. Do not take for granted the Earth and its elements. Earth is in charge of your entire existence. Listen and learn how it works, not to control it, but to be guided by it.

Good vs. Evil

All man-made religions rely on the battle between good and evil. There is the epitome-of-good place, where the god lives, called heaven or such. Then there is the epitome-of-evil place where the devil-guy lives, called hell or such. The devil is the antithesis of the god and the main cause of all the bad stuff that happens, according to the religion. They offer their idea of goodness as a solution and a healing salve to the evil that exists in their world. If there were no evil, they would have no 'product' to sell, so they keep making the flock feel guilty for doing and thinking evil stuff. They are in constant war against evil, even though they are also the creators of the evil, which they constantly renew and keep fresh in the minds of the flock. If evil disappeared, they would be out of business. So they have to refresh the sense of evil in the minds of the flock so the flock must turn to the religion to be saved from the evil. The contrived efficiency of this man-made scam is the contradictory nature that makes the flock feel like helpless pawns, being pulled in opposing directions by the forces of good and evil, in a never-ending struggle for truth, justice, peace, comfort, etc., which leads them to seek help from the shepherd, the same shepherd that put them on that roller coaster of a life as soon as they joined the flock.

This process reinforces the personal conflict against the evil-guy in the minds of the flock so they realize their helplessness, shame, guilt, and desperate need for the salvation that can only be achieved through participation in the flock, all the while not allowing the flock to question the religion's authority or seek real truth elsewhere, for fear the flock might actually learn truth, grow beyond the naive mind set the religion enforces, and achieve some mature intellectual strength and ability. Like when a child is afraid of the dark, and their parents hug them and tell them everything is okay, and put them back into bed with a teddy-bear or such to hold onto. The child has learned nothing about the darkness except that if they hold onto this security blanket everything feels better. It does not resolve the problem and only treats a symptom on a superficial, emotional level. To really help the child learn about darkness, they should turn on some light and show them that there is nothing there in the dark that is not there in the light and that darkness is just the absence of light, the same as closing their eyes while playing a game. This works very well unless the child is being taught about the devil in Sunday school, which creates a warped perception of the real world. Many shepherds consider it proper control to scare children into a fear that only they can comfort, if only superficially.

By creating a problem that can only be resolved by the cure that the religions are selling, they are able to build and maintain a captive consumer base. They sell the related therapies that require continuous attendance and cash donations, so they can reinforce the need for the cure as well as the problem that requires the cure. This type of cycle goes on for a lifetime. It is like a condition. It never gets cured, but is constantly being treated. Once the treatment is stopped, the condition goes away. It is like being treated by a doctor. Most doctors want to treat patients, not cure them. It would weaken their income base. Most medicine creates more problems, requiring more treatment, more medicine, more problems, more treatment, and so on as long as the money holds out.

If the sacred text says that god forgives the evil stuff the flock does, and the flock is saved by accepting the salvation thrust upon them by god, why should they be concerned about the evil? Since evil and good cannot exist in the same place at the same time, according to the text, then the saved no longer need the salvation from the shepherds. Saved is saved. Or is it?

Since the god's son died for the purpose of saving everyone, why must they constantly seek to be saved? If a flock member is saved by the grace of the god then why do the shepherds keep reminding and insisting that the flocks are such horrible sinners? Can a saved person be a sinner? Which part of their program is real, the grace that saves, or the evil that condemns? It's a trick question. Neither is real, and any way you look at it, the sheep get caught in the middle. Surely the grace, being from the god, should be eternal and forever and, as a gift from god, never be revocable. But the shepherds contradict, saying the flock must seek the grace/salvation every day and every moment of every day which means the gifts from god are overcome by the realities of daily living and therefore whatever the sheep are doing is more powerful than the grace and salvation that comes from god. This shows that the god is less powerful than the sheep, because the god is only a concept injected into the minds of the sheep and reinforced by the shepherds who keep the flocks off balance by requiring the flocks to get their daily fix of salvation, and by relying on the shepherds to get it for them.

Rather than admit that man is more powerful than the god, the shepherds blame the devil and his crew for the evil that infects man, which is giving the devil more power than god and makes humans the weakest link in the process. So the shepherds keep the fight for the control of humankind between god and the devil and they set themselves up as the brave defenders of humankind against the forces of evil, with the sheep as the prize to the winner. Wait a minute...!!

Is not the god the all-powerful, all-knowing, all-everything and therefore the most powerful force? So how can humans keep needing the salvation that is freely given to everyone by god? Surely god is not taking back this wonderful gift every time it is given just so the shepherds have something to do by telling the flock to seek god's goodness so that all the gifts of grace and salvation will be theirs forever, just to have it revoked again so they can seek it again. This concept is so flawed, it is obviously a man-made scam. It is less real than the daily soap operas where the characters are always creating new emotional roller coasters. The contradictory nature of the teachings is further stimulated by the concept that the devil is constantly at work disrupting the good in the world. The devil, also a man-made concept, is part of the package. It keeps the problem fresh and the need for resolution just as fresh. It all takes place in the minds of the flock members, from the highest shepherd to the most newly fleeced member of the flock. As long as they can keep the flock emotionally on edge, the fleecer wins, the sheep lose.

The shepherds, especially the evangelists, and worst of all, the TV evangelists and other flock fleecers, will create scenarios that are scarier than the worst nightmares ever on Elm or any other street. They will scrape at the sorest spot to get the flocks attention then remind them of the deepest dread fears surrounding them constantly. Then, after the flock is thoroughly uncomfortable, they will wring out of them every last comforting thought and filet the remaining bit of hope. Once the crowd is whipped into a frenzy of doubt and fear, the fleecer will tell them that the way to remove these fears and be free from the maladies that threaten is to accept his version of god's solution, which requires the sheep to give themselves over to god thru him and trust in his translation of god's plan for their lives, and buy the book he just happens to be selling (copies are available in back of the temple at the 'money-changers' tables). The plan involves emptying their wallet into the offering plate, doing as they are told without questioning the god's wisdom as presented thru the fleecer, and being a regular fleecee by participating in the programs set forth by the god but administrated by the fleecer, who talks with the god directly and often.

Flock's money + the fleecer's program = apparent salvation.

The fleecers give a lifetime guarantee of the truth of what they say because, unless the flock wakes up and smells what the fleecer is shoveling, no one will ever know the truth until they have died, at which moment they will realize they were lied to since they were children. But it's already too late! They closed the lid on their coffin. Since there is no proof available to the living, there are no dissatisfied customers, except those who have learned to listen with their brain rather than their emotions.

The sheep are taught to turn the other cheek, face evil with good, the meek shall inherit the earth, and other such sugar-coated niceties. Shepherds teach this ploy to keep the sheep docile and passive, and less likely to run or fight in response to the demands of the shepherd. This same type of passive attitude allowed the extermination of so many thousands during WWII. Is there anyone who has not seen the films of large groups being herded toward their doom by just a handful of guards with rifles? Had they fought back against their exterminators and attacked the few guards that prodded them toward their death, many more of them would have survived and a lot more bad guys would have died, and the outcome would have been more evenly distributed.

By relying on the power of fear for so many centuries to control their flocks, the shepherds have made the sheep afraid and quick to cower at the first hint of violence. This allows the hijackers and terrorists a big advantage when they make their move to inflict fear upon a community. The sheep do what they do best...nothing, or even worse...they comply.

The Earth is a good place. When it shrugs and a lot of sheep are killed it is usually due to mans interference. If man had not sold ocean front property to the sheep, they would not have had their house washed away. Earth needs to be respected, not feared. When Earth shrugs, it usually overwhelms man and his buildings, because man has not yet learned to respect Earth and those areas where the shrugs are prone to occur.

Obedience

It is more than just esprit de corps. It is blind, faithful allegiance to the will of the religion, the shepherds, and all the constructed 'truths', which are often confusing and contradictory. The obedience is crucial to the shepherd's control of the flock and the survival of the religion. The combination of fear, guilt, and peer pressure keep the flock coming back to get a regular fix of courage and forgiveness, only to be reminded of the things that they are supposed to fear and the reasons to feel guilty. The superstitious sense of fear and guilt offset by the artificial sense of courage and forgiveness create a cycle of need/fulfillment, as well as a sense of confusion and contrariness, leading to feelings of desperation, which is to be comforted by the message of love and the sense of belonging. The cycle continues with the religion insisting that it is the only solution for these problems; problems that it created in the first place, which they blame on the evils of the world around them. The flock seeks solutions and solace and in exchange give up their freedom and become obedient to the will of the religion.

Humans are born free, and yet, everywhere they turn, some flock or other is putting restrictions or controls on their actions and thoughts; from political parties, HMO's, AARP, unions, corporations, and clubs, to name a few. The most influential of these are the man-made religions because most people are born into one or the other of them, and they have never thought to question the validity or truth of the fundamental beliefs.... it has always been accepted as truth and that was that. They have come to believe that questioning is a sign of disobedience, lacking in faith and being unworthy or outside of the flock: the chosen, the holy, the saved, yadda, yadda, yadda, etc.

The rules are taught and repeated throughout the life of the flock. Many of them are simple and straight-forward. But some are twisted or spun into controlling demands, further dulling the sheep's ability to think except as robots, reprogramming their personal choices to reflect the choices of the religion. Many of the rules are constructed of confusing and contradictory truths which form the foundation of the religion's creed. Obedience is a path of many obstacles.

Requiring the sheep to confess their weaknesses and shortcomings to a shepherd is a good way to find out what the sheep are thinking and doing when they are outside the reach of the shepherd, and it puts them in the humiliating position of being constantly under the control of the shepherd, as though the shepherd is always looking over their shoulder, further reinforcing the fear and guilt levels. The same system reinforces in the sheep the notion that they can do whatever they desire because they have no responsibility for their behavior and no sense of discipline for behavior. It is the shepherds job to enforce the god's will upon them as the god directs. The sheep have developed through generations of historical habituation a severe lack of personal discipline and personal responsibility. They have only to behave as directed, and if they 'err' or 'sin' they are forgiven by the god, according to the shepherd. They go through life as irresponsible, undisciplined, non-thinking sheep.

The shepherds must never let the sheep think they can talk directly to the god and ask for forgiveness, they would miss out on all the great gossip. And by keeping in touch with the community grapevine, they are able to see more of the pieces of the whole, giving them an exceptional advantage of knowing more than any other member of the community. They must maintain the processes whereby they reinforce their superiority and control over the sheep, giving the shepherd an emotional advantage over the flock so they will do his bidding, not to mention the powerful opportunity to discover who would be the easiest to manipulate into a compromising situation of blackmail, molestation or even rape.

Earth does not require obedience, but it does have limits within which you need to function if you plan to live and survive. The limits are easily learned once they are seen and understood, but beyond their bounds one finds a very unforgiving Earth. When Earth shrugs: hurricane, tsunami, tornado, cyclone, earthquake, volcanic eruption, forest/wild fire, drought, flood, extreme heat/cold, etc: everything is completely at the mercy of the energy being released. Man still thinks he is in charge of the planet and continues to ignore the ways of the Earth and continues to suffer the consequences. There is no intercession by any shepherd, or any other representative of the religions who can in any way lessen the results or lower the body count when the shrug is over. There is only the Earth and it abides by the laws of physics and chemistry. For example: Earth is not just going through a strange weather cycle due to pollution. It is, however, still thawing out from the last ice age that ended over 10,000 years ago. Humans cannot comprehend the multi-century scope of such a cycle, and human pollution contributes to the process, and humans refuse to learn to not pollute or abuse the Earth, exacerbating the process.

Even though Earth is absorbing and reversing some pollution, it will not be able to maintain a humanly survivable atmosphere until the pollution stops or humans die off. After which the planet will regenerate and restore itself over a multi-century rehabilitation process and be ready for the next inhabitants to develop and start another civilization. When the tenants are not responsible, the landlord evicts them and finds new tenants that will care for and respect the property. Earth is not responsible to humans to maintain anything that allows them to continue to survive. We may be experiencing the only cycle of Earth atmosphere that happens to be inhabitable for these past few hundreds of thousands of years. The tenants are responsible for maintaining the atmosphere and conditions as they found them. The human developed over hundreds of thousands of years of specie survival and extinction to become the genetic combination of chemistry and physics that survived and thrived, and through their own ego-centric stubbornness promoted by the man made religions, humans are able to cause their own extinction in just a few centuries.

Until humans learn to work with the Earth and support its ways, they will be the unwelcome fleas infesting the planet, and it is only a matter of time before the Earth shrugs one last time and they all disappear.

Experience

Miracles are events described by someone who heard about it from someone else who did not see it either.

All man-made religions emphasize and focus upon the experiential aspects, so the emotional feeling blends with the physical doing of the rituals to produce a sense of harmony and well-being that attaches to the pseudo-spiritual values presented in the text and expounded upon during the repetitive meetings and indoctrination sessions, to create a feeling that reinforces the power of the words. Regular and repetitive doses of rousing sermons and emotionally charged performances with provocative music and audience participation, makes a person feel uplifted, just like the euphoric 'high' experienced by a heroin addict who just got fixed. The euphoric feelings are defined as salvation by the members of the flock, and when combined with the guilt trips that the shepherds enforce upon them at the meetings, it becomes a cycle of religious experience…going from the low of feeling worthless and/or guilty, to the high of feeling saved and purified. Religious rituals, prayers, and meetings all reinforce the propaganda and mind-control to maintain a controlling level of intrusion into the lives of those caught up in the historical habituation of being members of the flock.

When children are sentenced to life in a man-made religion their life is focused upon the superstitious myths and fantasies through which they must now filter all the input the world is throwing at them. As they grow up, they find that the world becomes a dichotomous, even schizophrenic, experience between the real world of school, play, work, and secular peer pressure that appears totally different from the world of superstition, myth and flock peer pressure that their religion forces them to use to figure out what pose they should imitate for each changing situation that pops up in their life. They seek but cannot find any helpful examples among the shepherds of the flocks who are more like out-of-work actors, seldom dealing with hard reality, putting everything on a subjective level, teaching behaviors rather than thought processes, and coercion rather than free-thinking decision, as they get the flock worked up into an agreeable and charitable mood just before they pass the offering plates.

Religions have developed the process into a corporate lifestyle. By maintaining the myths of hope for the hopeless, love for the unloved, empowerment for the weak, help for the helpless, and whatever for the whateverless, all things for all people, the religions maintain their cash flow. As long as the superstitious myths are repetitively reinforced they will continue as if they were true and maintain their strangle hold on the fears and guilt of the flocks, permitting the religions to continue to spin the webs of deceit and peer pressure. The blind faithful will continue to be awed by the smoke and mirrors, dog and pony shows of the sacraments and rituals, and they will return next week to be awed all over again by a similar routine. It is a spiral cycle of blind faith, smoke and mirrors, peer pressure, and flock mentality, all paid for by the flock.

If you live with those who fear, you will learn to be afraid.

For centuries of generations the sheep have lived in the shadow of the shepherds and have learned naught but to rely on their religion to guide their lives: the blind and lame leading the blinder and lamer. After a broken leg is healed, the person need no longer limp nor rely on a crutch, once they have learned to walk again on their own. The sheep never walk without the crutch, and they cannot see or understand truth or reality.

A flock member cannot realize nor understand the emptiness and phoniness of a man-made religion until they withdraw from it long enough for the repetitious, programmed propaganda to stop ringing in their ears and echoing in their mind, and stimulating their emotions. Since all of their programming has been a combination of actions and emotions with no thinking reality, only that which feels real as the emotion sweeps over them. They need to go through a withdrawal period to severe the Pavlovian stimulus/response connection which has been solidly reinforced for as long as they have been a member of the flock. They have been performing to the shepherd's tune for so long that, even if they do quit, they will automatically head for church on Sunday mornings for a few weeks until it has a chance to wear off, and they have some opportunities to think for themselves for a change. Only then will they have an opportunity to think freely and clearly, maybe for the first time in their life.

The sheep are kept from thinking by the constant reinforcement of the complete reliance upon the god to take care of everything as translated and taught by the shepherd. The sheep live very docile lives, following the flock, waiting for the god to tell the shepherd what to do and how to do, covering all aspects of their lives. It is like the sheep are at the oars of a large galley. All they do is propel the ship with no thought or decision about where it goes. The main shepherd is steering and other shepherds are cracking the whips to get as much out of the sheep as possible without killing them. The sheep just go with the flow and rely on the shepherds to guide the operation, as they are directed by the god. They must not rock the boat, just keep it going, relying on others to make all the decisions for them. It is easy to see how so much of America has gotten so fat and lazy because they are a part of the man-made religions that have turned them into sheep for so many generations that they no longer realize how pathetic they are. The flock mentality that began in the early Middle Ages is at fault. So many generations have succumbed to the brain-numbing effects of the man-made religions, that much of the world is populated by sheep and controlled by the shepherds, keeping the flocks blissfully unaware that a problem even exists. The world is under the control of those who are happy to take greedy advantage of the sheep, abusing them and the planet for their personal gain.

When the sheep have been historically habituated for so long into accepting as truth, and feeling that they believe, all the myth-laden propaganda and constructed history that has been repeatedly reinforced in their mind since childhood, their response to leaving is fear. Fear of the unknown, seemingly cold, non-sugar-coated reality that they believe is outside the flocks embrace and will harm them, makes them want to stay in the cozy comfort of the myth-filled constructs that have been their security blanket for their entire life. It requires a bold step to wean oneself away from that which has been a combination of security blanket and blinders for as long as they can remember. Until one has the courage to step away from the historically habituated routine to look at, listen to, and try to understand the truth of the real world, they will continue in blissful ignorance and prideful arrogance; deaf, dumb, and blind to the real world, as they continue to follow, swallow, and support the greatest charade of all: man-made religions.

By experiencing the Earth and learning to understand it, one can become one with the Earth, respecting its control of all aspects of life and learning to go with the flow.

Knowing

All man-made religions construct a sense of knowing, in spite of there being few or no facts to actually provide a foundation of knowledge. Though it is abstract and speculative, and based on subjective, emotional responses, it has been around for so long that it has become historically habituated into the generations. Telling a story, especially a big lie, loud enough and long enough, tends to make it accepted as truth. The abundance of such repetitive rhetoric, over the centuries, with the reinforcement of empirical places and dates where similar things may have actually happened, but have no foundation in fact, have resulted in an accepted historical record which is part of the invented, but accepted, 'knowledge'.

All of the sheep learn to think the same way as the rest of the flock, beginning with the first days of Sunday school, as soon as the child is old enough to speak and learn to repeat memorized phrases and wear cute outfits without diapers. Their mental process is molded to the way of the religion so everything is filtered as it gets funneled thru the self-centered, subjective set of beliefs, resulting in a very narrow, managed type of knowledge, a controlled pathway thru which all incoming data must flow and be processed. Actually it is more of a gauntlet that tears at any new truth and bends it to fit the mindset of the flock, creating a simple, narrow band of invented and spun-into truth that conforms to the fundamental beliefs of the religion. These religions thrive on the fact that they have brainwashed so many generations of scared and insecure sheep into accepting and believing the superstitious dinosaur dumplings that they are shoveling down their throats, that the flock is made to feel guilty if they should read or think about any alternative to those established beliefs.

Consider the analogy of a person who lived, restrained by bindings, in a cave, so they were facing away from the opening all their life and had never seen the world outside, except for the occasional shadow that was cast upon the wall when someone walked past the cave's entrance. Their knowledge of the world, their sense of reality, would be limited to what they had experienced within the scope of their very limited world view, only knowing what was available within the limits imposed by the environment. They would probably think the world was two dimensional, without color or language, and until they take some initiative, break their bonds, and turn away from the wall and the limited vision of the cave, and walk outside into the sunshine and fresh air, they will remain uninformed about the rest of the real world. The lives of flock members is similarly limited, since the only truth they are allowed to know is that which is filtered through the system of beliefs they are forced to swallow and follow, and they are unaware of the controlling bonds that bind them. They do not know that they do not know. If a color blind person does not know they are color-blind, the world seems to be just fine, until they try to cross the intersection against the light.

Many of the flock actually believe that they are saved. Some will say that they know they are saved as if that makes it stronger.

When actually they talk about it in order to feel better about it, convincing themselves that their naive fantasy is true. This sense of salvation frees them to do as they please since they believe their god has already chosen them and forgiven them for everything they have ever done or will ever do, and keeps them safe from all evil. They feel this further guarantees them a place next to their god when their physical life ends. This is their life's goal, their epitome of perfection and happiness. The problem with this kind of knowing is that their faith in and reliance upon the god's effect on their lives makes them very naive to the real world around them, and they rely on prayer instead of common sense to resolve problems, trusting in their god rather than using rational thought to make a decision based upon real facts.

Their sense of eternal salvation, in whatever form, as a part of their religion's package, tends to make the saved members of the flock more irresponsible toward others. It is a most perfect last stop on the ultimate ego trip: a very self-centered, ego-oriented, self-serving goal that is firmly etched into the brains of the "chosen". They become more egocentric, if that's possible, more disrespectful of others rights and more insistent on having things their way. Many of the holier-than-thou rise to the uppermost level as part of the governing board of the flock where they start making policy that controls the behavior of the entire flock. It becomes their 'heaven-on-earth' wherein they are a god, a head shepherd, in control of the flock, the ultimate ego trip. Many feel they are partners with their god so they are no longer answerable to anyone but their god for their actions.

This same sense of religious fervor and self-righteousness has been responsible for the deaths of thousands upon thousands of people all over the world. From the Inquisition, which was begun in 1233, by Pope Gregory IX, and was finally suppressed in 1820, finishing its "sacred work" by 1830's just to make it an even 600 yrs of killing, torture and abuse sanctioned by the church. The Crusades: from 1095 to 1396, lots of dead sheep on both sides, and the ego-driven barbaric behavior of the crusaders turned Moslem against Christian to the current day, and many others, like the Witch hunts, or the Mormon massacre, etc., just to list a few. All the holier-than-thou(s) killing people because of their subjective sense of religious indignation and intolerance that no one involved really understood or remembers. People who profess to being totally dedicated to their god seem very anxious to inflict their ideals and creeds upon others who already have a set of beliefs that work just fine for them. Many of the 'saved' feel that no matter what they do in their life on this planet, they will be completely exonerated and rewarded after their death because they were chosen by their god, giving no thought to the fact that their religion was invented by man, centuries ago, to control the naive populations of the ancient world. They feel they are forgiven and saved because they supported all the creeds and rituals of their religion, and they are 'chosen'.

Eternal life is an oxymoron. Life is a cycle which includes death and decomposition, which supports new life, starting all over at the bottom of the food chain. Except that for the past hundreds of years, bodies are buried in boxes inside of cement tombs that are sealed off from the natural chemical process that renews the earth and the food chain. The burial practices have been around for generations and have been promoted by the religions which enjoy selling a ritual every chance they get. But the notion of being raised to eternal life includes the concept of regaining the use of the body at resurrection (Fourth Lateran Council 1215 AD, Pope Innocent III), the same way that the religion's messenger allegedly did after his death, according to Paul's text. The man-made religions support the practice of burying dead bodies in sealed boxes to copy the entombment of their idol, who was resurrected whole according to their religious beliefs. During the burial ritual they say things like "ashes to ashes and dust to dust" or "from the dust you were born and to the dust you shall return" but, ironically, they prevent it by entombing the body. This keeps the body from returning to its elements and disrupts the chemical balance of the Earth. Small wonder the farmers have to use more and more chemicals to grow their crops. So many centuries of this practice has depleted the natural balance of the food chain. Worms have more to do with less raw material. The Pauline myth about after-life, is just another of the many superstitions that the sheep were led to believe since they were kids. Dead is dead. A life that was little or no contribution to this world while alive, should at least contribute to the food chain as it decomposes.

The Church of Rome has a unique twist on the after life. It used to be called indulgence; a process whereby the church could remove any punishment the deceased may face in the hereafter for the payment of extra works around the church by the relatives; a good source of free labor or whatever (!), or by payment in cash. They have convinced the flock that the dearly departed has entered into a process that will require lots of prayers, masses, and money to help the departed get thru the journey and arrive at heaven, and these masses and prayer cards are conveniently purchased thru any of their churches.

Learning about and becoming one with the Earth is knowledge of reality, born of rational thought and use of your mental capacities to understand and embrace the energies that drive and guide the Earth and all of the universe.

True Knowledge

Why is it so difficult for the sheep to see beyond the shepherd? Self-conceit. It is impossible for anyone to begin to learn truth when they think they already possess it, and the shepherd continuously confirms and reinforces this falsehood so he won't lose out on the regular fleecings. The sheep are kept ignorant of their ignorance.

An old Arabian saying from an anonymous writer speaks volumes:

He who knows not, and knows not he knows not,

he is a fool; shun him.

He who knows not, and knows he knows not,

he is ignorant; teach him.

He who knows, and knows not he knows,

he is asleep; awaken him.

But he who knows, and knows he knows,

he is wise; follow him.

All of the shepherds that I have ever heard, seen, or met, were members of the first category. But with their egocentric bravado, they appear to be of the last category. They consider themselves to be of the last level since their egos make them think they are speaking the truth that comes from real knowledge because that is the level of naivety where they exist, when actually they do not know that they do not know the truth. It has been unavailable to them because they cannot think outside of the flock mentality. They have believed in the same superstitious fantasy world all of their lives and have known nothing else. These are the fools of the world and are the most dangerous purveyors of superstitions and other falsehoods in exchange for money, blindly given by those seeking peace and salvation. They think they are in the final category and represent themselves as such, giving false hope and false information to those who trust them, in exchange for their personal prosperity.

Most politicians are just such shepherds. Their inability to recognize or speak truth has been historically habituated in their psyche since they grew up as sheep and have been fed so much spun-out-of-shape rhetoric for so many generations. They do not know what truth is. They cannot recognize it behind the distortions that are spouted at them by so many spin-speakers. The distortions have become the "truth" and the spiral of spin-speaking continues on its downward path, degenerating towards retardation of a nation, so that, finally, no child is left behind because all have succumbed to the mind-numbing will of the shepherds. There is no longer any standard of truth, intelligence, or integrity in America, the shepherds have seen to it that the sheep do not and will not recognize the truth even when presented in plain language.

Some well-known Infidels…and other purveyors of truth…

Christianity and the other man-made religions have always managed to kill off, hide and/or down-play their critics, making it appear that the religions are in the majority and the skeptics are just wrong or 'lost'. The truth is that those who refuse to be misled by the spin-speaking shepherds of the man-made religions are just quieter and content to watch the priestcraft in their fancy robes and funny hats, parade about, in all their pretended piety and profound godliness as they preach about what their god said to them just last night. Many of these who live outside of the flock mentality do believe in a higher power, not the superstitious, irrational fantasies revealed by the shepherd's visions that give them the sacred authority to control and direct the sheep of the flocks, but that which stands up to reason and critical inquiry as it reveals truth.

Opposition to the superstition-filled, irrational Christianity grew during the Renaissance, the Age of Reason, and especially through the scientific revolution of the 19th and 20th centuries. Voltaire saw religion as a club to wield over the heads of the masses. John Locke felt that reason must be in control. Feuerbach taught that god was a product of human imagination. Nietzsche professed that god was dead and that Christianity resented the world, the body, sex, critical intelligence and everything strong and healthy, and that it created a slave mentality. Freud considered religion to be a psychological delusion. Karl Marx referred to religion as the opiate of the masses, describing very accurately so many who cannot go without their weekly, or, in some cases, daily fix of the reinforcing flock mentality. Thomas Paine, in "The Age of Reason" (1794 – 1795), called the colonial alliance of church and state an "adulterous connection" and a tyranny from which men must be rescued. Many politicians have tried to induce the sheep into just such an alliance.

After the Civil War in America, Robert Ingersoll (1833 – 1899) was considered the 'national infidel' because he argued that science and reason exposed the contradictory and shadowy nature of Christianity that was obvious to any who could think for themselves, and that religion was the enemy of the people, that leads to "softening of the brain and an ossification of the heart." In the thirties, H. L. Mencken and Clarence Darrow, condemned religion as a flight from reality. But to those who are so deeply caught in the web of deceit and superstitious indoctrination, it has become their reality.

My reality was formed and informed by being raised as a preacher's kid, with all that can possibly include, and being totally swept up into the Christian phenomena, completing seminary with a Master of Divinity and shepherding a few flocks. I had been so caught up in the phenomena that my entire being was deeply committed to it. Then I had an opportunity to see and hear and think outside of the constraints of the flocks, and my mind hit the brakes. I was stunned by the eye-opening fact that I did not know what I did not know, and I set about to find it.

I realized that I had been acting the role of shepherd, and my entire professional career had been a lie up to that point. There was a thinking, intelligent person inside that would always follow the real Jesus with his message of peace and love, but could no longer pretend to accept and blindly follow the Pauline Christianity that demands blind faith in the superstitious man-made mythology and invented theology that the mythical Paul, the Holy Roman Empire, and the Roman Catholic Church used to create the Christian religion. My professional success within this phenomena also required my allegiance to the man-made political structure of the particular church, which further restricted freedom and free thought. I had seen, heard, felt, tasted, and swallowed enough of the dinosaur dumplings that these two forces were shoveling at me, and it offended me to think I had been an instrument of such falsehood to so many sheep.

After I escaped from the yoke of the oppressors, I felt somewhat off-balance and bewildered. I had never viewed the world without the flock filters, and the experience was both liberating and a bit frightening. Experiencing the world as it really is, without the sugar-coated propaganda ringing in my ears, and without the flock or the shepherds quoting their superstitious security blanket of parroted phrases, let me use my rational intelligence to find my way.

It was only after his retirement that my dad, a Christian pastor his entire adult life, and I had a chance to discuss the lack of truth in religion. It was during these talks that he expressed a sincere sense of disillusionment in the superstitious falsehoods and machinations of religion and the ministry. By the time of our talks, he had been out of the shepherd business for about seven years, and the façade was wearing off and reality was getting clearer. A hard thing to face after a lifetime of service to a god which he finally realized was a supernatural fantasy. He had always been a very devout man of his faith, which always came first, before even his family. He accepted that he had actually been in the first category, because he realized that he had not known that he had not known the truth, only the man-made constructs which he had taught and preached with great enthusiasm as though they were the absolute truth. Our talks centered around what was really real; the elements, a sense of oneness with nature, an awareness of the omnipotence of energy and the universe, and how by combining these intellectually, without spinning or twisting, we arrived at a point that was not unlike that of the ancient pagans. We realized that the Earth and the elements were showing us where the ultimate power resided.

The profundity of the concept prompted us to visit England, the home of our ancestors, and the center of ancient pagan sites, including Stonehenge. It was a powerful, eye-opening experience to see and feel the wisdom and intellect that went into such a massive structure honoring the Earth. We also enjoyed the contrast of the modern Druids who came to be seen at the site: parading their pretended piety of their man-made morphed Christian/Druidry, prancing about, wearing all sorts of symbols and emblems on their fancy robes, and funny hats on their apparently empty heads. Man-made religions are a world-wide circus parade, enticing the sheep to follow them to the main attraction.

There came a most enlightening and liberating understanding of how everything is alive because the energy of the atom that is in everything that exists is what drives the universe, giving everything life. The fire in the atom is the life force within all things. Energy is life.

The Earth is a living entity, growing, changing, reproducing itself, supporting life, giving shelter, feeding the inhabitants, and punishing those who fail to understand the ways of the elements, which combine to form the universe; the Earth in particular. In this, we discovered the true expression of the 'prime mover' was the Earth. The comprehension of this was very liberating and gave a sense of freedom and openness, replacing the shackles of man-made religion with a new understanding of the true essence of man and what that means. Man's place in the world is limited only by what he is able to understand about the world around him. The sheep of the flocks continue believing the sugar-coated, fantasy world, magical mystery tour that they have swallowed and followed all their life, and are blissfully unaware of the real world.

The single thing that pervades all of the universe is the energy which holds it together. This is the "omnipotent oneness" that man has sought for so long. It lives in every molecule of earth, air, fire, and water at the atomic level. The entire universe is interconnected because of this interrelationship of the electrical/atomic energy common to all things. The Chinese have a similar understanding that they refer to as "Chi", which refers to the life force that is within each person, and in all things. It refers to balance and harmony as well as power and gentleness. The electrical energy of the atom is just such a force.

The atomic structure is the format for the universe, from the sub-atomic particles among the protons and electrons of every atom of matter to the comets and asteroids among the planets revolving around the Suns throughout the galaxies of the universe. Our Milky Way Galaxy may be a mere sub-atomic sized particle among the electrons revolving within an atom of hydrogen in the water of someone's bathtub on another plane of existence that we cannot even comprehend.

All that exists is made of this energy, like the spark of thought which travels across neural synapses to enable us to have and to understand thoughts and ideas. That micro-spark is the substance of which ideas are formed as they travel across the neurons bringing micro-bytes together to form concepts. The ideas are never destroyed, and often they are re-interpreted by someone else whose neurons picked up the signal and they carry on where others have left off.

The intellect and wisdom of the universe is contained in and controlled by this energy, a constant that does not die, but occurs in different forms, and is always in motion, like a fiery spark. Thought and wisdom live in the universe powered by this same energy: the living, omnipotent oneness that controls the universe.

Here is the omnipotent and omniscient; the 'prime mover' that all the naïve, self-centered theologians can only think of in personified terms as their divine grandfather-type being, hovering overhead, which they plan to become when they are resurrected. It is time to burst the self-indulgent, bellicose bubbles of flock-fed flatulence of these power-hungry shepherds. The totally objective, guiding power of the universe is the electrical/atomic energy that is in everything.

It seems so simple in its complexity, and complex in its simplicity. It takes whatever form serves its purpose, as vast as all the elements of the Earth.

Energy is the sacred entity. Without it nothing exists. Everything that exists does so because of the atomic energy within it, which gives it life, form, and function. If you must worship something, this energy is worthy of your reverence and respect, not thru a bunch of mindless rituals and repetitive statements, but with your mind; your main source of this energy. Seek to understand and become one with it, not to control it, but to be guided by it.

Meditation is one way to get in touch with the energy of the universe. Meditation is more than prayer, it is a matter of focus and honesty. True seekers must learn to focus, not on the imaginary grandfather in the sky that they have prayed to all their life, but on the energy within their mind. Spoken words are not necessary. Be concise and clear, because the energy within the mind will guide the process. The mind's mental energy is the most powerful force for the good of mind and body. It is more than just mind over matter. It is the way to heal body and mind. It is the access terminal to the power of the universe. As people do more of it, they will find they become more a part of the flow of life, and they discover the peace and tranquility of letting the universal energy include them in the flow of life.

When someone starts to understand and become one with the elements, their knowledge blossoms as they start to see how they fit into this amazing universe. As they embrace the elements of the universe, they become more synchronized to the rhythm of the living universe, and they start to experience oneness with the elements and eventually with the universe. Mental and emotional oneness with the Earth energy leads to an ability to synchronize oneself with the Earth and soon find circumstances going your same way. Much like tuning in the exact frequency of a radio so you hear the fullness of the music. When you get on the same level of understanding of and reverence for the Earth, our closest connection to the entire universe, you soon find you can communicate with the energy. At first in small ways, like knowing what the weather will be by just paying attention to it. Then in more interesting ways, like when you do something, out of the ordinary, for no apparent reason, only to find that it kept you from physical harm; and your health improves, and the flow of life around you seems to be going your way. Soon you realize the Earth-centered energy is all around you, and you are aware of it and able to understand more and more. As you become more focused on the Earth energy, you learn and understand more and you become more in 'sync' with the Earth.

Earth energy is in control of life on this planet, not men and their ego-centric, invented religions, with their man-made rituals and routines. Earth does not respond to such trivialities. Imagine trying to stop a tsunami with prayer beads, or a forest fire with a papal bull, or a tornado with a rosary, a hurricane with a crucifix. There are enough centuries of proof that it just does not work. Never has. Never will. When Earth shrugs, man-made religion is, as always, totally impotent.

Those who continue to be misled by the self-absorbed shepherds, whose only agenda is to collect more tax-free money from the sheep as they lead them in the fulfillment of the shepherds' prosperity, continue to receive a lot of empty promises, hollow feelings, and phoniness, that is very impressively veiled behind fancy robes, funny hats, huge glass and gold cathedrals, elaborate stage shows, and lots of man-made rules and requirements, all for the edification of the shepherds, paid for by the sheep. Earth focus is not a religion. It is a way of life. It can become your way of life, once you realize the awesome power and wisdom of it. There is no worship place to attend. The Earth is all around you. Find a spot that man has not yet abused and enjoy your journey toward synchronicity with the Earth. There are no rituals or canned prayers, no peer pressure or offering plates. No superstitious magical mystery tour... Only the peace and serenity of the Earth energy.

Feel the flow of the energy and the harmony all around you;
the balance and unity,
the power and the gentleness.
Welcome to truth,
understanding,
real knowledge,
and real life.

Enjoy!

The Elements

The universe is made up of four basic elements; air, fire, earth, and water, and a few hundred specific elements such as hydrogen and oxygen, all powered by the electrical spark of life; atomic energy. For many millennia the most brilliant philosophers and theologians, members of different flocks, have sought to identify the "prime mover" of all things, so they can further personify and clarify the concept and make it more marketable to the flocks. They have come up with all sorts of religious statements, decrees, dogma, and papal bull (emphasis on the bull), all pointing toward a single source of all that exists. But since they cannot see it objectively, only subjectively, all they can do is personify the notion of a deity. They are constrained, by their religion, to keep falling back on the kindly 'grandfather in the sky' concept of the prime mover. Since they have not the capacity for rational objective thought due to their being mired in the superstitious quagmire of their own making, they will not be able to understand the reality of the elements. The four basic elements are the main building blocks of everything that exists, and the electrical energy that powers the atom is the ultimate essence that makes it all operate, gives it life, form and function.

The Earth is the proper representation of all that is omnipotent, omniscient, and all whatever, anywhere and everywhere. It is the essence of power, strength, wisdom, and life. The ancient Druids (10,000 +/- B.C.) had the right relationship with the Earth: they respected and revered it so much that they worshipped it. Their oral traditions; poems, songs and stories were very similar in subject and tone to the Psalms and Song of Solomon from the Christian Bible.

Over time their worship practices got more and more ritually elaborate as they became more and more compromised by some priest-types practicing their priestcraft on the naive, for their own personal prosperity. But the basic premise still holds true: the Druids were known as the Earth-worshipping, tree-huggers, and well-versed in the use of poetry and song to express their devotion.

Other examples of element worship from history was an Egyptian group that worshipped the Sun as their god, or the American Indians, who worshipped the Earth and the elements, because they knew their lives depended upon them. Historical records indicate that most religions were centered around worship of an idol or some invisible, personified deity, and was centered around the temples and the shepherds who had the flocks wrapped around their little fingers right next to their fancy rings and bells.

The Earth should be a focus of reverence and respect, as should the elements as the messengers of the Earth. The messages are loud and clear if they are heeded. For example: To avoid loss of life and as an expression of respect for the Earth and life; do not build homes along the San Andreas Fault, around active volcanoes, or on stilts along the unstable coastline. Do not build flammable houses among trees and shrubbery that is flammable in areas prone to drought and flood cycles just because it looks quaint or because it is what everybody else is doing. Do not under estimate the power of a tidal wave or tsunami, it cannot be outrun. Even in a tie, you lose.

When the Earth shrugs, the entire planet must pay attention. No amount of prayer, ritual, sacrament, or priestcraft can reduce the body count. It has nothing to do with your god "moving in mysterious ways" or "god's ways are not known to man." That is the oldest and foulest form of dinosaur dumplings that was ever invented to explain away that which the ignorant mind cannot understand. The man-made gods have nothing to do with it and are powerless to stop, slow, or control any of it. But it provides the shepherds with grand opportunities to collect more money and implant more fear and sell more comfort as their god moves in mysterious ways.

These natural catastrophes are understandable and, when monitored, can be less devastating. But to do that there needs to be developed among the population of the Earth a serious respect and reverence for the Earth and the elements, and at the center of it all, an understanding of the energy of the atom as the prime mover, and life-giver/taker. With so much about this planet that the sciences are just starting to understand, it seems a waste of money to spend billions to explore other planets until we have learned all we can about Earth. Not the least of which should be spent to protect this planet from the abuse, pollution and other contamination that the sheep have forced into the environment, because their god said they were in charge of and supposed to dominate the Earth. The misguided man-made religions have done more damage than good to the Earth.

When the Earth shrugs, mountains are torn apart, lava flows, the crust renews and rebuilds itself, flexing and stretching, expanding and contracting, breaking down and building up. Creating and renewing, Woe to those who get in the way.

When the wind blows, clearing and cleansing the pollution from the air, churning and refreshing the seas, moving the deserts, humbling the architects and builders, blowing where it wills.

When the water flows, wearing down and building up, renewing the layers of nutrition for the plants and animals that rely upon it, able to neutralize some human pollution, not restrained by boundaries, supporting life. It flows and ebbs with the rhythm of the Earth.

The fire of the Sun warms and supports life. The lightning freshens the air, prunes the forests, goes where it wills, and reminds man that he is not in control. The fire from within the Earth renews the surface, creates new land, buries the old, giving the Earth a face-lift and tummy-tuck all at the same time.

The strongest and largest of man's structures are subject to the forces of the Earth, as are the greatest trees and mountains. Humans must become more aware of and seek to understand more about the living Earth, or we risk extinction for failure to learn about, honor and respect the uniqueness and power of the Earth. It is not sacred because it is holy or magical or any such man-made dinosaur dumplings, but because we depend upon it for our very existence. It must be considered the most precious thing beyond all that man could ever imagine, and yet, humans take it for granted as they continue to abuse and misuse the elements as though they were in charge and have an unlimited supply of everything.

It is easy to learn about the elements by using the abilities with which you were born. Watch, listen, smell, taste, feel, and most important, think.

Listen to the wind as it whispers about the upcoming weather. The birds are screaming about it, telling all who can hear and understand, their lives depend upon it. Sometimes it speaks in whispers, sometimes in great and deafening howls and groans.

Watch the water as it ebbs and flows, contemplate its motion, feel its energy. It is the only thing on the planet that cannot be compressed. From the smallest brook to the largest tsunami, the fog that quiets as it hangs in the air, the morning dew on the grass, the condensate on your cold glass of wine, the smallest pond, the largest ocean, all ebb and flow.

From the tiniest spark that transmits a thought from one neuron to another as your mind thinks, or the atom; held together by the interaction of the protons, neutrons, and electrons; the dancing flames of a campfire that warm, illuminate, and make s'mores; the powerful plume of lava spewing from the volcano, or the fierce flash of lightning that turns a mighty tree into toothpicks as it ignites a fire to thin the forest. It is amazing.

The Earth is alive, always changing yet almost always the same, giving shelter, food, water, warmth, comfort, and supporting life. It is a system of checks and balances that truly works. Like the seasons, the Earth is in constant motion, ebb and flow, hot and cold, wet and dry. The electrical charges build up to a point where they seek resolution in a discharge of energy that resolves into neutrality, only to build up again and continue the cycle.

SOME ALTERNATIVE TEXT

The Psalms of the Bible are so like the oral traditions of the early Druids that it is easy to see a great deal of similarity. Could they have been adopted by the early writers of the biblical text to fit their agenda? With a bit of word substitution, it is quite easy to see the Earth as the object of many of the Psalms, Proverbs, or Song of Solomon, representing the prime mover: atomic energy.

Earth version of Psalm 23.

The Earth is my shepherd, I have no wants.
I lie down in green pastures, finding shelter and food.
Warmed by the Sun, energized to move and enjoy life.
Breathing warm sweet air, swept clean by the winds and the trees,
sustaining my being.
Drinking the water that cleanses my body, inside and out,
restoring my vital essence.
Showing me the ways of life that lead to harmony,
Remaining steadfast to the flow of life processes,
in spite of the carelessness of others,
who think only of themselves and follow false gods,
weakening the quality of life they might otherwise know.
Providing for all my needs, even when others wish me harm,
Pouring positive support over me throughout my life;
I will keep my heart centered in the Earth, and live joyfully in
its embrace forever.

Proverbs 1.

That men may know wisdom and instruction, understand words of insight, receive instruction in wise dealing, righteousness, justice, and equity; that prudence may be given to the simple, knowledge and discretion to the youth, the wise man may also hear and increase in learning, and the man of understanding acquire skill, to understand a proverb and a figure, the words of the wise and their riddles.

Learning of the Earth is the beginning of knowledge; fools despise wisdom and instruction.

Hear, my son, your father's instruction and reject not your mother's teaching; for they will comfort and protect you.

My son, if evil ones entice you, do not agree.

If they say," Come with us to shed the blood of the innocent and take their precious goods, so we will have abundance". Do not follow their path. Their path leads to their own destruction. Such is the way of those who know not that they know not, and abuse those who know not and know not that they know not.

The Earth cries aloud in the villages and coastlines, and within the city gates;

"How long, O simple ones, will you love being simple?

How long will scorners delight in their scorning and fools hate knowledge?

Give heed to my teaching; behold, I will pour out my knowledge to you; I will make my knowledge known to you.

Because I have called and you refused to listen, reached out to you and you turned away, you ignored my counsel and my teaching,

The Earth laughs at your calamity, ignoring when panic strikes you, when panic strikes as a storm, and disaster comes as a hurricane, earthquake or tsunami, when distress and anguish tear at you.

Then you will seek to learn of and respect the Earth, in vain, and you will have to suffer the consequences for your failure to learn the ways of the Earth.

For the sheep are killed by ignoring the lessons, and the conceit of the shepherds condemns them.

But those who learn the ways of the Earth will dwell secure and will be at ease, with no fear."

Psalm 24.

The Earth is the life-giving essence, all of it is sacred, as are the wonders of it and all that lives within its life-giving forces.

Who will endure and continue to thrive, living in comfort?

Those who respect and honor the Earth,
Who do not abuse, misuse, and contaminate, while spinning
lies into truth to cover their evilness.
They will thrive and live comfortably who respect and honor
the Earth.
The Earth is the great sacred one.
Open your eyes and your mind.
The Earth is the great essence.

Psalm 25.

To you, great Earth, I dedicate my essence.

You only do I trust, you always give me positive support.

I trust the Earth and am always proud to do so.

Those who abuse the Earth will not escape the effect.

Those who abuse the Earth will live in chaos.

Great Earth, Teach me your ways.

Help me learn true harmony.

Knowledge of your truth is real strength.

The careless ways of my youth were often foolish and harmful.

But Earth's forgiving steadfastness upheld me.

Those who truly seek to understand truth are able to learn the harmony of the Earth.

The life-giving harmony of Earth is constant and unfailing.

The way of Earth is life.

Those who understand the awesome truth of Earth will see the power of life there displayed…

Behold…. the awesome essence of Earth's truth:

Air cleanses and is the breath of life.

Fire renews and is the essential power of life.

Earth supports, shelters, giving life and constant renewal.

Water refreshes and supports the essence of life.

Energy keeps all in harmony, the essence of thought and understanding.

The Earth supports and protects those who understand its harmony.

The Earth-family bond is strong. The cycle is ever-flowing.

Truth leads to understanding which leads to real knowledge, which leads to real life.

Psalm 1.

Alive in truth is the person who shuns the wicked, avoids the mean-spirited and ego-driven, and turns away from the false-speakers, the spinners of truth.

The truly alive delight in real truth and the harmony of Earth; seeking to learn, to know, and to understand more; always more.

Like a tree growing near a stream. The water nourishes and feeds.

The air nourishes and cleanses. The Sun warms and energizes.

The Earth supports and feeds. The energy guides and informs.

In harmony with Earth, it is sustained, it grows, it yields fruit, and continues in the cycle of life.

Psalm 73

Earth is good to those who have learned the truth about reality.

When I lost my step and fell away from the true path, I pursued the prosperity of the wicked, looking away from the sanctity of the Earth.

I cared not for the future of the Earth, not realizing that it was also my future.

The wicked feel no guilt or sorrow as they waste and abuse the elements of the Earth. Their pride and arrogance carry them along. They understand nothing about the elements.

Their violence is concealed behind elegant facades while the environment struggles to recover.

Their eyes look only for more profit, more ease, and more riches. Their hearts are hardened as they grow fatter.

Their folly deepens as they scoff and speak malicious lofty words. They no longer recognize truth, and their existence threatens the Earth.

The unknowing masses praise the wicked because they see only the vastness of their riches. They cannot see the even greater vastness of their evil.

The Earth knows and remembers; the scars inform and remind.

The unknowing are starting to see and becoming informed.

The scars upon the Earth are plentiful, and they remind all who care and understand.

Earth beatitudes: 'Ifs' for real life.

If you feel deflated and empty; let the Sun warm your face, let the Earth caress your weary body, and the wind refresh your tired lungs. Refocus away from yourself, toward the living Earth around you.

If you mourn the loss of loved ones; know that they are still in the Earth-family. Their energy does not die. Feel their energy from the Earth.

If you are calm-spirited and slow to anger: You will more easily learn the peaceful way of Earth-life and Earth-knowledge, and find the harmony of Earth.

If you actively seek true knowledge and understanding, you will find it. The road will be long and hard, and filled with spinners of false truth.

If you seek truth, pure and uncontaminated: be ready to give up the security blankets of your youth, and you can find the harmony of Earth and become a member of its family, and find true peace and security.

For Those Who Must Have Rules:
An Earth-Friendly Top Ten

1. The Earth is the ONLY PLANET supporting life, as we know. Respect and honor it above all else, or GET OFF!

2. Base your life in reality, not superstition. Man-made religions and their gods are not real. If man made it how can it be greater than man?

3. Do not abuse or misuse the Earth or anything that dwells upon it. Be responsible for your actions and those of your children, and the results of them.

4. Take time to experience and understand the Earth, and the elements; air, fire, earth, and water. Think more, worry less.

5. Children: respect and honor your parents. Parents: respect and honor your children. Teach, comfort, and care for each other. You reflect each other.

6. Respect and cherish all life. Life begins at independent survival. Death begins at dependent survival.

7. The union of two essences is to be honored and respected.

8. You cannot have that which you have not earned. If you have not earned it, it is not yours. If it is not yours, you cannot have it. You are not owed anything that you have not earned.

9. If it is not the real truth, do not say it is. Truth heals and uplifts. Falsehood creates suffering and decay. Avoid liars and spin-speakers, they contaminate the world. If it sounds too good to be true, it is not true.

10. Become one with the elements and the Earth, and the rest will fall into place.

I hope this has stimulated your desire to learn, think, and decide for yourself.

There are many more places to look.

This only scratches the surface.

You've only just begun!

Ask....
    search....
        grow....
           seek....
              learn...

                  and

                    keep growing!!!!!!

References: where names, dates and quotes referred to herein were lifted, these sources, among others...many were published before 1900.

Adams, G. B., *Civilization During the Middle Ages.*, Scribners, NY.

Addis,W.E. and Arnold, Thomas, *A Catholic Dictionary*, containing some account of the Doctrine, Discipline, Rites, Ceremonies, Councils, and Religious Orders of the Catholic Church. London.

Alzog, John, *Manual of Universal Church History.* 3 volumes. Cincinnati.

Balzani, Ugo, *The Popes and the Hohenstaufen.* Epochs of Church History, NY.

Be'mont, Charles and Monod, G., *Medieval Europe, 395-1270.* Holt, NY.

Belloc, H. *Robespierre*, NY.

Bullfinch, Thomas, *Charlemagne, or Romance of the Middle Ages.* Edited by A.R. Marsh. Boston.

Burckhardt, Jacob, *The Civilization of the Renaissance in Italy*, NY.

Brauer, Jerald C., Ed. *Westminster Dictionary of Church History*, Phila, PA.

Church, A.J., *The Beginning of the Middle Ages*, (Epochs) NY.

Cox, G. W., *The Crusades*, (Epochs) NY.

Cuts, E. L., *Turning Points of General Church History.* London.

Duruy, Victor, *History of the Middle Ages.* NY.

Emerton, Ephraim, *Medieval Europe, 814-1300.* Ginn.

Ferm, Vergilius, Ed,. *An Encyclopedia of Religion.* NY.

Fischer, G. P., *History of the Christian Church.* NY.

Fisher, Herbert, *The Medieval Empire.* 2vol. NY.

Gibbon, Edward, *The History of the Decline and Fall of the Roman Empire.* J.B.Bury, Ed. 7 vol. London.

Guizot, F. P. G., *History of Civilization.* 4 vol. (Bohn) NY.

Harding, S. B., *Essentials in Medieval and Modern History.* London, 1905.

Henderson, E. F., *Select Historical Documents of the Middle Ages*. NY.

Keary, C. F., *The Vikings in Western Christendom*. NY.

Lacroix, Paul, *Military and Religious Life in the Middle Ages*. London.

Lea, H. C., *History of the Inquisition of the Middle Ages*. 3 vol. Phila. PA.

Milman, H. H., *History of Latin Christianity*. 4 vol. NY.

Mombert, J. I., *A Short History of the Crusades*. NY.

Munro, D. C. & Sellery, G. C., (ed), *Medieval Civilization: Selected Studies from European Authors, translated and edited*. NY.

Oman, C. W. C., *The Dark Ages, 476-918*. (Periods) NY.

Pastor, Ludwig, *History of the Popes*. 6 vol. London, St.Louis.

Schaff-Herzog, *Religious Encyclopoedia.*, 4 vol. NY.

Tout, T. F., *The Empire and the Papacy, 918-1273*. (Periods) NY.

Trench, R. C., *Lectures on Medieval Church History*. NY.